READERS THEATRE

Dickenson Titles of Related Interest

Acting: The Creative Process
Second Edition
Hardie Albright

The Director Prepares
Stanley L. Glenn

The Challenge of the Theatre:
An Introduction to Drama
J.L. Styan

Stage Direction in Transition
Hardie Albright

Scenebook for Student Actors
Ruth Lane

READERS THEATRE

Jerry V. Pickering

California State University, Fullerton

Dickenson Publishing Company, Inc.
Encino, California
Belmont, California

Copyright © 1975 by Dickenson Publishing Company, Inc. All rights reserved. No part of this book may be reproduced, stored in a retrieval system, or transcribed, in any form or by any means—electronic, mechanical, photocopying, recording, or otherwise—without the prior written permission of the publisher, 16561 Ventura Boulevard, Encino, California 91316.

ISBN-0-8221-0135-1
Library of Congress Catalog Card Number: 74-83952
Printed in the United States of America
Printing (last digit): 9 8 7 6 5 4 3 2 1

PN
4145
.P47

Contents

Preface — vii

1. Definitions of Readers Theatre — 1
2. The Current Revival — 8
3. Selecting the Literature — 19
4. Adapting the Literature — 32
5. Creating the Original Script — 43
6. Script Analysis — 52
7. Casting — 59
8. Directing — 68
9. Rehearsals and Performance — 93

Readers Theatre Scripts

Headaches, Heartaches, and Innocence Be Damned — 101

Elijah — 123

The Farce of Master Pierre Pathelin — 137

Suggested Sources for Readers Theatre Production Material — 167

Notes — 175

Index — 177

Preface

Some people say—and I fully agree—that directing or performing in a Readers Theatre production is one of the most exciting and rewarding ventures that a man or woman can undertake. Readers Theatre has almost no limits, dealing in an artistic way with all literature of all time. True, it requires exacting craftsmanship and an incisive critical approach, but the end result is not merely to dissect and classify the literary work, but to free it from the confines of the printed page and allow it to achieve those heights that only the imagination is capable of reaching.

For their help in making this book possible, I want to thank my colleagues in the Theatre Department, California State University, Fullerton. I have learned much about the art and craft of theatre in all its forms from their generous advice and comments. I also wish to thank the several reviewers whose suggestions have so altered this book, from its first draft to this final, printed form: Professors Kathleen Bindert, California State University, Northridge; Janet Bolton, University of Southern California; Jack Holland, Orange Coast College; Keith Laing, Citrus College; S. J. Macksoud, State University of New York, Binghamton; Robert Reynolds, Moorpark Junior College; and Alan Stambusky, University of California, Davis.

I also wish to acknowledge the following people and institutions: Dr. Douglas McDermott, director, for permission to publish photographs of his production of *Under Milk Wood*, produced at the University of California, Davis, by the Department of Dramatic Art;

Dr. Alvin Keller, chairman, Theatre Department, California State University, Fullerton, for permission to publish photographs of *Dracula,* directed by Dr. Robert Rence; *The Glass Managerie,* directed by Dr. Donald Henry; *Major Barbara* and *Once in a Lifetime,* directed by Dr. Alvin Keller; and "A Reading of T. S. Eliot's Poetry," directed by Dr. LaNor Lollich;

Mr. William Purkiss, Orange Coast College, for permission to publish photographs of his productions of *John Brown's Body, The World of Carl Sandburg,* and "Profiles of Man";

Mr. Charles Redmon, Jr., photographer, and Ms. Paula Dinkel and Mr. Ron Matthews, models, for permission to print the photographs illustrating stage position; and

Mr. Verne Thomas, for his help and advice when this book was barely underway.

I am grateful for permission to reprint from the following material:

Headaches, Heartaches, and Innocence Be Damned by Dr. Ronald K. Dieb, copyright © 1973 by Ronald K. Dieb; printed with permission of the author; and

"Ten Indians" by Ernest Hemingway; reprinted from *Men Without Women* by Ernest Hemingway. Copyright 1927 by Charles Scribner's Sons, by Ernest Hemingway; used by permission of the publishers.

I am grateful to the Yale University Press for permission to reprint an excerpt from *Long Day's Journey Into Night* by Eugene O'Neill, copyright © 1955 by Carlotta Monterey O'Neill.

I especially wish to thank my wife for her help and support, and for putting up with me while I was writing this book.

JERRY V. PICKERING

CHAPTER 1

Definitions of Readers Theatre

An audience is seated in a small theatre. The curtains are up, revealing a stage that is bare except for the platforms that provide three playing levels. The houselights are up full and Russian music is playing faintly in the background.

The houselights dim to one-half and the music rises. Three people, two men and a woman, enter from stage right. Each carries a light wooden reading stool and a music stand on which is a script in a black-covered, loose-leaf binder. The stools and stands are arranged on the platforms; the performers take seats on the stools, their heads down.

The houselights and stage lights go dark and the music fades.

The stage lights come up, with area lighting defining each of the reading positions.

Reader 1 stands and, as Narrator, reads. . . .

> The tiny and extraordinarily skinny peasant, wearing patched pants and a shirt of striped linen, stood facing the investigating magistrate. His hairy face was pitted with smallpox, and his eyes, scarcely visible under overhanging brows, conveyed an expression of sullen resentment. He wore his hair in a tangled, unkempt thatch which somehow emphasized his sullen, spiderlike character. He was barefoot.[1]

A Readers Theatre presentation of Anton Chekhov's short story, "The Malefactor," has begun.

Any attempt to completely define or pigeonhole Readers Theatre faces enormous problems from the very start, for the medium is flexible and should not be restricted by such peremptory treatment. Readers Theatre, as an art form, is a hybrid, with roots in both oral interpretation and conventional theatre. It combines the best of both these mediums, but is not limited by the conventions of either. This fortunate freedom from convention has allowed Readers Theatre to grow and develop as an art.

Though Readers Theatre or something very like it stretches back into the antiquity of the performing arts, the wide-ranging possibilities that this form of theatre offers had never been fully realized or explored. However, such realization and exploration are now underway. After a long hiatus Readers Theatre has been rediscovered, to the delight of both performers and audiences, for it provides a vehicle for experimentation in theatrical forms. It offers a method for presenting to audiences not only the traditional works of dramatic literature, but perhaps more importantly, those vast, formerly untouched areas of nondramatic literature.

READERS THEATRE AND CONVENTIONAL THEATRE

Unlike conventional drama, where the emphasis has long been divided between the *action* and the *dialogue,* Readers Theatre emphasizes the *text.* In terms of conventional theatre, the text often exists only as a plan for physical or dramatic action; for Readers Theatre, the text *is* the action. With minimal (or nonexistent) attention to historically accurate costuming, and with simplified lighting and scenery, Readers Theatre focuses audience attention directly on the author's creation.

Because of this emphasis on text, and because Readers Theatre has tended to become involved primarily in the presentation of literary, nondramatic works, with a minimum of theatrical trappings, certain philosophical and physical traditions have evolved. Philosophically, the intent of Readers Theatre is to "feature" a text; that is, to illuminate, clarify, and display the specific literary work being presented. This means, in fact, to suggest vocally and physically not only the text but the subtext as defined through close critical analysis. It also means a minimizing of such traditional ingredients of production as physical action, scenery, costumes, and props. For these reasons, Readers Theatre has come to depend on reading from a manuscript that is usually present (and often completely visible) on stage, and on making obvious use of such physical properties as reading stands and stools.

Perhaps the main difference between conventional theatre and Readers Theatre is that the latter makes no attempt to create reality "on stage." Whereas conventional theatre, through the use of complete action, sets, and costumes, often asks the audience to believe for the duration of the performance that certain characters do exist in reality on stage, Readers Theatre, through suggested action and minimal staging, attempts to bring the author's creation alive in the mind of the audience. Out of this attempt grows one of the most important concepts of Readers Theatre: that in most cases the action is not on stage with the readers, but "out front," in the mind of the audience.

THE AUDIENCE AS PERFORMER-CREATOR

Implicit in the concept of the action taking place in the mind of the audience is the belief that the audience, by providing the scene of the action (and to some degree the characterization), is as much involved in the performance as the readers. The idea of audience participation in the drama is hardly a new one, though in terms of the traditional drama this participation has tended to be vicarious. However, in the case of Readers Theatre, where the largest part of the action takes place in the mind of the audience, the audience actually becomes *performer* rather than vicarious participant, and the whole concept of performance must be expanded to include "audience performance." In the fullest sense, then, the audience becomes performer-creator, with the mind receiving the material and hints given by the readers, and the fancy operating in the creative sense that both Coleridge and Pirandello, among others, have envisioned.

READERS THEATRE AND ORAL INTERPRETATION

But if Readers Theatre is not just a scaled-down version of conventional theatre, neither is it merely a group effort at oral interpretation, though it is more closely related to this art than it is to the traditional stage. If oral interpretation is, as Charlotte I. Lee insists, a single artist revivifying one art through another, much "as a musician translates the written notes into sound and thus conveys the achievement of the composer to the listener,"[2] then Readers Theatre stands somewhat outside that special art in the sense that it is a group effort in which the performers often make use of limited theatrical techniques and materials to aid the audience in imaginatively bringing a total work of literature to life.

EDUCATIONAL READERS THEATRE

While it is easy enough to say what Readers Theatre is *not*, definitions of what it *is* do not come easily. Perhaps this is because the art is such a flexible one, able to deal with a vast range of literary material, and perhaps it is because the material itself shapes the usages to which it will be put. In either case, this lack of formal definition is probably to the good, for any art that is too rigidly formulated—squeezed tightly into the spaces between strict rules—is unlikely to achieve continuing creative development.

From Tennessee Williams's *Glass Menagerie.* The physical separation of the readers, lit by tight spots and surrounded by darkness, is used to suggest the spiritual isolation of Williams's characters.

However, to gain the fullest possible understanding of the state of the art as it exists today—both as an indicator of potential direction for future development, and as an operational basis for current production—some basic (though not too structured) definition is needed. For this purpose, a look at the range of existing definitions may be helpful, for by taking them into account it is possible to arrive at a basic definition that is, if not final, at least comprehensive and workable.

One of the most complete definitions (and an operational one) has been provided by Marion L. and Marvin D. Kleinau. They identify Readers Theatre as being any production containing two or more readers, each assigned to an individual role or roles, and each engaged in the art of presenting a literary work to an audience through the medium of oral interpretation. A single reader may perform several roles, or two or more readers may voice the same line in unison. This definition, though not fully comprehensive, has the virtue of describing what is nearly always found in a Readers Theatre production and thus defines that which can be physically verified. It goes on to point out that the scene of the action in Readers Theatre must be set in the abstract, or in the minds of the audience members. That is, the scene never becomes the concrete area of "the stage," as it does in conventional theatrical production.[3]

Wallace Bacon, taking a rather specific approach to the subject, has stated that Readers Theatre "embraces the group reading of material involving delineated characters, with or without the presence of a narrator, in such a manner as to establish the focus of the piece not on stage with the actor-readers, but in the imagination of the audience."[4]

In the opinion of Leslie I. Coger and Melvin R. White, the largest part of Readers Theatre action does not occur on stage with the interpreter but, rather, in the imagination of the audience. Thus, the audience "is stimulated to experience the emotional impact of the literature as well as its intellectual content, and since so much of the performance depends on the mental creativity and contribution of the audience, Readers Theatre may well be called the theatre of the mind."[5]

As a final example of definition we may turn to Keith Brooks, who offers the following: "Readers Theatre is a group activity in which the best of literature is communicated from manuscript to an audience through the oral interpretation approach of vocal and physical suggestion."[6]

From the preceding definitions, primarily by people who operate in the field of educational theatre, several points may be abstracted: (1) Readers Theatre is the oral presentation of literature to an audience, (2) by two or more readers, (3) utilizing primarily the techniques of oral interpretation, (4) in a manner that locates the scene in the imaginations of the audience members, (5) thus stimulating them to use their own imaginative facility in the re-creation of the literary work.

PROFESSIONAL READERS THEATRE

Along with its extensive use by educational theatre groups, Readers Theatre has enjoyed a substantial professional success, especially in such urban areas as New York, where production costs have soared, making traditional theatre a highly expensive proposition. For the contemporary period, major professional Readers Theatre began its career on October 22, 1951, when Charles Laughton, Agnes Moorehead, Charles Boyer, and Sir Cedric Hardwicke gave a highly acclaimed interpretative reading of George Bernard Shaw's *Don Juan in Hell.* The production enjoyed a successful tour, receiving the plaudits of audiences and critics all over the country. Following this production, Readers Theatre soon established itself as a commercial-professional medium with great potential, which is still in the process of realization.

Critical reviews of professional Readers Theatre productions in New York have been studied by Keith Brooks and John Bielenberg.[7] Together they analyzed reviews of fourteen professional productions in an attempt to define

From G. B. Shaw's *Major Barbara*. The production utilized fully authentic costume, make-up, and some set decoration.

the major aspects of professional Readers Theatre. The productions were investigated in terms of the type of literature presented, the reactions of critics and audience to the readers, the techniques of presentation employed, and the various aspects of staging.

Interestingly, the forte of the professional Readers Theatre in New York, just as in educational theatre all over the country, turned out to be the presentation of works from nondramatic literature. With a few exceptions, such as *Don Juan in Hell* and John Gielgud's *Ages of Man* (which was made up of selections from many plays), we find readings of nondramatic material from such diverse writers as Sean O'Casey, Oscar Wilde, Carl Sandburg, Mark Twain, Charles Dickens, Stephen Vincent Benét, and Bertolt Brecht. If one compares them to the writers whose works are usually found on the Broadway stage, the value of Readers Theatre becomes immediately apparent.

There is no accurate method available for measuring audience reaction to the reader. However, the New York drama critics felt that the audience certainly responded to the skill of the reader as well as to the material presented and, further, that the average playgoer would rather hear poor literature brilliantly read than brilliant literature poorly read.

Investigation of the techniques employed by the professionals indicated that certain basic minimums do exist, although a rather considerable variety of techniques have been put to use. First, the programs were billed as *readings* and not as plays. Second, in every case the actual text was present and visible on stage as a symbol of both the source and the approach, whether the performers actually read from it or not. Third, the readers did without most of the physical accoutrements of the traditional stage, usually locating themselves on stools behind lecterns. Fourth, in most cases the readers made no attempt to become the characters they were reading. Fifth, costume was usually formal evening wear. Finally, most readers presented numerous characters.

Physically the professional productions tended to follow the pattern of scenic simplicity established by the Paul Gregory production of *Don Juan in Hell*. In most cases the basic elements were high stools and lecterns, set in front of a neutral background, and aided by subtle and often complex lighting techniques to enhance the mood and to help shift focus from one reader to another or to help emphasize the change when a single reader moved from one characterization into another. Music, like light, was often an integral part of the performances, and as such received favorable reaction from critics and audience alike. In fact, the carefully conceived use of lighting and music made the traditional scenic decor quite unnecessary.

From this study of professional Readers Theatre a number of points may be abstracted and combined into a working definition of the medium. These are: (1) The material is drawn primarily from nondramatic literature; (2) the text is usually present on stage; (3) most of the physical accoutrements of the traditional theatre stage are eliminated; (4) subtle lighting is used; (5) music may be employed and, in fact, can be a valuable addition to the production; (6) costume is usually limited to formal evening wear; (7) reading stools and lecterns are used; (8) each reader portrays one or more characters; and (9) the basic physical concept of the show is one of scenic austerity and simplicity.

The philosophic difference between educational and professional Readers Theatre is almost nonexistent. The prime difference seems to be that educational Readers Theatre is deeply committed to defining that which already exists and experimenting to discover that which had never existed before, while professional Readers Theatre is less concerned with definitions and the purely educational experiment. For the professional, what is *good* can be defined as what *works*.

Perhaps the most valuable result of defining both educational and professional Readers Theatre is not the discovery of their many similarities—that could be assumed—but of their differences. If the scholarly and experimental approach of educational Readers Theatre could be married to the pragmatic approach of the professional groups, something very fine could be the result.

CHAPTER 2

The Current Revival

The advent of talking movies, the growing popularity of radio, the depression of the 1930s, and then World War II and its immediate aftermath, managed to put an end to any major form of Readers Theatre for nearly twenty-four years. This is not to say that Readers Theatre totally died out during this period, but activity was so severely curtailed that, when it was finally revived, it seemed to most critics to be almost a new medium. To some degree this reaction came about because the revival, when it did come, was not the result of a slow resurgence which would have allowed the critics time to examine the medium and its roots and discover that it merely represented one more phase of something that had been with us for many years. Instead, Readers Theatre exploded onto the national scene with a production conceived by one of our most imaginative producers and featuring four of the finest performers on the professional stage.

PROFESSIONAL PRODUCTIONS

This explosion occurred in February, 1951, at Claremont, California, with the initial production of *Don Juan in Hell,* the third act of George Bernard Shaw's *Man and Superman.* It was performed by a quartet of readers—Charles Laughton, Agnes Moorehead, Charles Boyer, and Sir Cedric Hardwicke—under the direction of Laughton. The original tour of the play ran through one hundred and five stops in thirty-five states, and the critical and audience reaction to these performances can easily be summed up in the reaction of the critic with the *New York World Telegram and Sun:* "Brilliant!"

The idea for the drama quartet was first conceived by Paul Gregory, who became producer of the company, leaving the direction of the show to Charles Laughton. Fortunately for audiences, Laughton was more than equal to the task. He created a clean, direct, formally presented show: in essence, classical. It consisted of four readers (including himself), a stage manager, and one crew-member. This allowed for a simple, uncluttered performance, with each reader taking only one role, and for a set that was simple in the extreme—four reading stools, music stands (because of the symphonic nature of the work), and microphones. The mikes served three purposes: They kept the actors in place; they provided the requisite volume for large audiences in auditoriums where acoustics were bad; and they allowed the performers to attain recognizable vocal levels.[1] The readers all wore evening dress.

The material was not, in fact, *read* in the sense that the title "Readers Theatre" implies. It had been carefully memorized even before the Quartet began rehearsal; this was especially necessary for Charles Boyer, who had more lines than Hamlet. Thus, the reading stands and scripts were utilized as props, and were kept constantly on view to remind the audience that this was, indeed, a performance of a written, literary work.[2]

Following the enormous success of *Don Juan in Hell,* the team of Gregory and Laughton continued their Readers Theatre endeavors with a production of Stephen Vincent Benét's long, narrative poem, *John Brown's Body.* The production opened on February 14, 1953, at the New Century Theatre in New York City. Again the direction was by Laughton; this time, however, there was music (and effects) by Walter Schumann, and choral direction by Richard White. Cast members were Tyrone Power, Judith Anderson, and Raymond Massey, plus a choral group that provided such special effects as chanting, humming, and movement, and which, like its Greek archetype,

This set for Stephen Vincent Benet's *John Brown's Body* was designed to suggest a southern exterior, with the crossed flags of the Union and the Confederacy suggesting the period and symbolizing the basic conflict. There was no effort made at authentic costuming, but the women's costumes were selected to suggest the period.

helped to advance the action. Lighting was used to enhance the mood and create a "set." This time the critical reaction was not as unanimously favorable as it had been for *Don Juan in Hell.* The form was no longer "new," and thus critics could make specific demands on the production. In terms of Readers Theatre, perhaps the highest critical acclaim was paid by reviewers John Chapman and William Hawkins, who pointed out that the staging was not intrusive and the production provoked the audience into forming their own mental images of the action.[3]

On September 16, 1956, after what amounted to a three-year hiatus for major Readers Theatre performances, Paul Shyre (producer and adapter) opened his production of *I Knock at the Door* at the 92nd Street YMHA in New York. It was based on the first volume of Sean O'Casey's three volume autobiography, and was the premiere production of a dramatic trilogy which would eventually include *Pictures in the Hallway* and *Drums Under the Window.* This production, directed by Stuart Vaughan, ran for nineteen performances and later reopened at the Phoenix Theatre in 1959 to run for eleven more nights. The concept in the first production of the trilogy (and later in the second) was that of concert reading, with the readers seated on stools behind lecterns. Each performer read several different parts. The cast, which included Staats Cotsworth, George Brenlin, Robert Gerringer, Rae Allen, and Paul Shyre, were praised for their ability to make the play "plug into life itself," but reviewers tended to find it a trifle confusing in that it failed to distinguish clearly between minor characters.[4] But if the first two parts of the trilogy were concert reading, the third part, *Drums Under the Window,* certainly was not. With the added perspective of several years, and the earlier two productions, Shyre decided to turn it into something resembling *concert theatre* as opposed to *concert reading.* There would be no pretense of reading from a text, and the physical action, while limited, would be an integral part of the concept. Seven actors would play a total of sixty roles, using the entire (and bare) stage to develop characterizations, and a narrator would link the thirty-two scenes.[5]

On October 15, 1957, a major contribution to Readers Theatre occurred with the opening of Dylan Thomas' *Under Milk Wood,* which the poet subtitled "A Play for Voices." Staged at Henry Miller's Theatre in New York, the play ran for thirty-nine performances. The cast, which included Sada Thompson, Dana Elcar, Jack Dodson, and Carol Teitel, merely read the poet's words, with minimal physical movement. The show was a critical success and underwent numerous revivals, one of the most interesting of which was the 1961 production, staged by William Ball at the Circle-in-the-Square, New York. Using a company of ten, seven of whom were in the original production, and a bare stage relieved only by a framework at one end of the playing area, Ball was applauded for bringing fluidity and contrast to the poet's constantly shifting images.[6]

A Readers Theatre production of Brecht's *Mother Courage*, beginning on October 12, 1959, kept the impetus of Readers Theatre alive and healthy in Los Angeles. The script, a two-act version of Brecht's play, was by Eric Bentley. It was presented in twelve scenes by the Theatre Group at Schoenberg Hall, University of California, Los Angeles, and ran for six performances. Produced and directed by Alan Cooke, the cast included Eileen Heckart, Charles Aidman, Jack Albertson, and Ross Martin. Again the set was reasonably simple, but this time scenic projections were used effectively to create a "set" onstage instead of purely in the imagination of the audience.

Even more important than *Mother Courage*, at least in terms of developing an audience for Readers Theatre, was the opening at the Martinique Theatre in New York of the highly successful *U.S.A.*, a reading production in two acts based on John Dos Passos' novel of the same name. It opened on October 28, twelve days after *Mother Courage* closed, and it ran for over 256 performances. Essentially the production was designed to present a dramatic commentary on various aspects of American life, from 1900 through the depression of the 1930s. It was directed by Dos Passos and Paul Shyre—fresh from his early stint with O'Casey—and featured six "newsmen," read by Laurence Hugo, William Windom, Peggy McCay, Joan Tetzel, William Redfield, and Sada Thompson. Technically, the production featured simple sets, with newsreels, orchestration, and fairly complex lighting to aid the "camera eye" stream of consciousness technique.[7]

The pace of professional Readers Theatre productions remained reasonably constant through the late 1950s. In 1960 the pace began to accelerate, though it hardly approached the rush of activity hoped for by a few aficionados. In that year the public was presented with such productions as *Drums Under the Window*, the third of Shyre's Readers Theatre adaptations of Sean O'Casey's autobiography, and *The World of Carl Sandburg*. In addition, there were major revivals of *John Brown's Body*, *I Knock at the Door*, and *Pictures in the Hallway* (these last two under the title *Two Evenings with Sean O'Casey*). In fact, throughout the 1960s the professional Readers Theatre programs became so numerous that discussion of each work is not only impossible but unnecessary. The general production format of the 1960s was much the same as the one established in the previous decade, with only a few exceptions, and it is with these exceptions that it is now necessary to deal.

The World of Carl Sandburg premiered at Henry Miller's Theatre on the evening of September 14, 1960, with an opening-night appearance by Sandburg himself, and ran through twenty-nine performances. The production, featuring Sandburg's deceptively simple homestyle prose and poetry, told the story of Man as he travels from the cradle to the grave. Adapted and directed by Norman Corwin, and read by Gary Merrill and Bette Davis, the work received only moderate praise from the critics. The bits of Sandburg's writing

12   The Current Revival

From Norman Corwin's *The World of Carl Sandburg*. This show was designed to travel and thus used only reading stools and such lighting as was available. Music was provided live by the performers (two guitarists and vocalists).

that Corwin had selected were damned as serviceable and sounding more than a bit like Biblical commentary. Gary Merrill's performance was called vigorous and direct, and Bette Davis was praised for having the good sense to give up her usual "high-styled authority" for a more human warmth. Successful as the production eventually turned out to be, with revivals on the professional stage, on numerous college campuses, and by community theatre groups, the most important thing about *Sandburg* was, perhaps, the presence onstage of Clark Allen, guitarist. Music had long been an essential part of Readers Theatre, provided by such means as onstage chorus or tape, and designed either to forward the material, to create mood and setting, or both. This time, however, because of Sandburg's own interest in American folk music, the songs were an integral part of the material itself and not merely supportive. *The World of Carl Sandburg* was, in essence, musical theatre, Readers Theatre style.

On January 3, 1962, at the Theatre de Lys in New York, the Gene Frankel directed production of *Brecht on Brecht* opened and subsequently ran for 440 performances, followed by a 55 performance run at the Sheridan Square Playhouse. The cast was particularly good, featuring Lotte Lenya, George Voskovec, Michael Wager, Dane Clark, Anne Jackson, and Viveca Lindfors. The program was divided into two parts (Part I titled "Life" and Part II titled "Theatre") and consisted of material from the songs, poems, letters, essays, stories, and plays by Brecht. The emphasis of the production was quite different from most Readers Theatre that had gone before; that is, instead of emphasizing the literary work it emphasized the poet in terms of his own works. This had already been done, to some extent, in Shyre's O'Casey productions, and in *Dear Liar,* but in both cases the artist was portrayed not through his great creative efforts but through autobiographical materials or through his letters. On the other hand, *The World of Carl Sandburg* emphasized not so much the poet, or his works, but the world of Man as filtered through the artistic consciousness of Sandburg. *Brecht on Brecht,* using both literary and nonliterary materials, concentrates directly on Brecht himself, attempting to explain him as a man, as an artist, as a philosopher, and, ultimately, as all three.

The 1963 season was especially memorable because of two productions. The first, a two-part concert reading of material from Edgar Lee Masters' *Spoon River Anthology,* was conceived by Charles Aidman and was first presented on May 1, 1963, in the Humanities Building Auditorium at the University of California, Los Angeles, by the Theatre Group. The cast included Betty Garrett, Robert Elston, Joyce Van Patten, Charles Aidman, Stephen Pearlman, and N. C. Hirshorn. The production was, essentially, an "out-of-town" tryout and its success was so encouraging that on September 29, 1963, it reopened at the Booth Theatre with only slight revisions. The set was a simple one, with four rough-looking benches for the readers, a lectern, and two seats at the side for the singers who performed Mr. Hirshorn's original songs. Again the production was well received and the *New York Times* eulogized that "although *Spoon River Anthology* never was meant for the stage, it has been transmitted into a glowing theatre experience."[8]

On October 31, 1963, in the Sheridan Square Playhouse, a cast that included Gloria Foster, James Greene, Moses Gunn, Claudette Nevins, Michael O'Sullivan, and Fred Pinkard, read various documents (with connecting narrative material) on the subject of the black man "in white America." The production, avoiding a growing tendency to give Readers Theatre a set and costumes nearly equivalent to fully staged drama, was directed by Harold Stone. The material, ranging freely through time and space, was given unity by the single thread of the black experience in America. Critics, on the whole, received the production with the reserved coolness that Martin Duberman's didacticism probably deserved: "*In White America* can laugh and mourn, but most of all it is filled with indignation...."[9] However, in spite of the generally unenthusiastic critical reception, the production went on to run for over 300 performances, with numerous professional and amateur revivals. In a sense, Readers Theatre came of age with *In White America* in that now, instead of concentrating purely on literature or makers of literature, it could use both literary and nonliterary materials to deal with contemporary social, moral, physical, and spiritual dilemmas. Readers Theatre, instead of being solely a method of displaying literary creation, had taken on the role of social commentator.

With this new set of credentials already firmly established, Readers Theatre continued its role of social critic when, on October 20, 1965, in the Volksbuhne Theatre in Berlin, Peter Weiss opened *The Investigation* to qualified praise from German critics. The work was exported and opened the 1966-67 season in New York City. This time it was somewhat more successful because material that was for the German audience an immediate accusation of guilt was for the American audience merely an uncomfortable reminder that they perhaps shared the guilt if they had not been active enough in social and political causes.

The production was, quite simply, an arrangement of excerpts from the transcript of the 1964-65 trial of those men who, at Auschwitz, between the years 1941 and 1945, had helped in some way to exterminate four million people. In choosing this material for Readers Theatre, Weiss provided for a major change in an artistic concept that had begun its resurgence on the premise of featuring a literary text. What *In White America* had done in large part, *The Investigation* did completely; that is, it used nonliterary materials to focus attention on a social and moral problem. In addition, the set—a multiple witness box placed in such a way that the spectators seemed to be sitting in the courtroom—provided a measure of realism previously unknown in Readers Theatre. The lighting increased the effect; the house-lights were left on during the production, which effectively turned the whole auditorium into a courtroom. There was no attempt to set a scene "out front" in the imagination of the audience, but to create a theatrical reality and make the audience an active part of that reality.

The American critical response was slightly more favorable than the German, but on the whole *The Investigation* succeeded neither as Readers Theatre nor as traditional, fully staged drama. It was, in fact, a major professional counterpart of the many hybrid forms already on the campuses.

The variety displayed by professional Readers Theatre, from 1951 to the present, in terms of style, performance, material, and even intent, has indeed been enormous. It has moved from a simple presentation of great literature, where the emphasis is "out front" and not on the performance or a specific performer, to a didactic social presentation where the material is completely nonliterary and the readers seek some identification with their roles in the manner of traditional stage drama. In such cases the action is not located in the mind of the audience; instead the audience is made an active participant. Between these extremes, the Readers Theatre directors have experimented with various combinations of literary and nonliterary materials, and with such traditional performance-related concepts as lighting, movement, composition, sound, and set design. From first to last it has been a medium of experimentation, perhaps the most experimental theatrical medium of this century. All that can be said with certainty is that the experimentation is far from over.

EDUCATIONAL THEATRE PRODUCTIONS

An assessment of the extent to which Readers Theatre existed on the university and college campuses during the 1950s and 60s is difficult to make because the records, except for major public performances, are generally incomplete. At the 1957 convention of the American Theatre Association, held jointly with the Speech Association of America, Helen Hicks of Hunter College presented Book I of Stephen Vincent Benét's *John Brown's Body*, with her readers sitting behind lecterns and reading from visible scripts. In 1960, at the annual convention of the Speech Association of America, Southwest Missouri State College presented an adaptation of Ray Bradbury's novel, *Dandelion Wine*. This production featured six readers using reading stools, lecterns, and limited movement. Other early productions were *Ebony Ghetto*, again by Southwest Missouri State College, *The Battle of the Sexes* by Central Michigan University; and Henry Fielding's *The Tragedy of Tragedies: Or, the Life and Death of Tom Thumb the Great* by Northwestern University.

The Speech Association of America, by way of the Interpretation Interest Group, has provided a generally good summary of work in the Readers Theatre field, in terms of performances and scholarly publications. Also, the more recent production lists of the American Theatre Association provide an interesting and quite informative view of what has happened, on an educational level, to Readers Theatre.

For the 1963-64 season, even though there was as yet no production breakdown for Readers Theatre, the production lists of the American Theatre Association reported that 370 plays were given as public readings.[10] In 1964-65 the number of public play readings grew to 475.[11] Finally, for the 1967-68 season, due to a growing demand, Readers Theatre was given a category of its own in the production lists.[12]

The most frequently produced writers for 1967-68 were Dylan Thomas, for *Under Milk Wood* and partially for his poetry, and Edgar Lee Masters for *Spoon River Anthology*. The rest of the list, after Thomas and Masters, were Norman Corwin *(The World of Carl Sandburg)*, T. S. Eliot, Ray Bradbury *(Dandelion Wine)*, Martin Duberman *(In White America)*, Tennessee Williams, George Bernard Shaw, and Edward Albee. The most often produced individual works were, as might be expected, *Spoon River Anthology, Under Milk Wood, Dandelion Wine, The World of Carl Sandburg, In White America, J. B.,* and *A Thurber Carnival*. While this is hardly an exhaustive list, it is indicative of directions in educational Readers Theatre and leads to some interesting conclusions. First, of the nine playwrights represented, the last three are men who have written only for legitimate or fully staged theatre. Also, of the top seven productions, the last two are works designed specifically for traditional

This scene from Dylan Thomas's *Under Milk Wood* shows a production done on a thrust stage, with two major levels, seven potential reading areas, and limited realistic movement.

stage production. The conclusion is inescapable that "play reading"—the interpretative reading of plays originally designed for full staging—is far more common at the college and university level than it is professionally. Secondly, the theory that Readers Theatre is a medium through which a broad, general selection of literature is featured, as opposed to the featuring of production values or specific performers, seems to receive a bit more lip service than actual practice. This becomes evident in the fact that of the top seven programs, the first five are fully written productions, though specifically designed for Readers Theatre performance, and not original literary materials put together by the director to provide an audience with a new and unique experience. The last two productions on the list, while particularly suited for Readers Theatre, are designed for traditional staging. Of the authors most produced, only one—T. S. Eliot—earned his position solely by his literary work and not because a prepackaged show of his materials was already available to the Readers Theatre director.

The seasons following 1967-68 have failed to appreciably change the university and college Readers Theatre production picture. Some of the selections do, of course, change. For example, the 1968-69 season featured two newcomers: George Orwell's *Animal Farm* (3rd place) and *John Brown's Body* (7th place). However, the list was again led by *Spoon River Anthology* and *Under Milk Wood,* and once more included *A Thurber Carnival* (4th place), *The World of Carl Sandburg* (5th place), and *In White America* (6th place).[13] The new additions, while welcome, hardly changed the earlier pattern. They are both complete shows and reflect the demand of Readers Theatre directors for prepackaged and, to some degree, presold shows.

While it is relatively easy, on one level, to fault the imagination and creativity of educational Readers Theatre programs, it must be remembered that the shows reported in most surveys of interpretative activity are major public productions and, as such, must compete for audiences with legitimate stage plays, films, television, and all the other artistic and entertainment offerings. There is, then, a reason for doing the big show, the "name" show, the show that was such a smash in New York. On the other hand, the productions that usually go unreported are the experimental works done in classrooms, in "brown bag" theatre, and for limited runs in evening productions. Reasons why such shows go unreported vary, from fears about their quality to fears regarding permissions and royalties. After all, how many classes can afford to pay royalties for performances given free of charge, on only two evenings, to very small audiences?

Educational institutions are, in fact, providing solid, creative, and highly imaginative work. Styles range from the clean, simple, essentially classic style, with readers seated on stools behind lecterns, to very complex productions which make maximum use of costume, lighting, sound, movement, and even set design to achieve their goals. Also, productions range in material from the purely literary to the totally nonliterary. The enormous range inherent in educational Readers Theatre can be seen by looking at three recent, representative productions.

In March, 1972, at the third Desert Interpretation Festival, sponsored by the University of Arizona, Professor LaNor Lollich of California State University, Fullerton, presented a highly successful reading of poems by T. S. Eliot. Her readers were dressed neatly in street clothes and were seated on reading stools, holding scripts in their hands. There was general area lighting and no "set." Movement was limited to simple changes in reading position and to the suggestive movement traditional to oral interpretation. Readers who were "off" simply bowed their heads. The success of this production, beyond the skill of the individual readers, rested primarily on its cleanness and simplicity which allowed full focus on Eliot's poetry.

In contrast, a student conceived, written, and directed production, based loosely on the transcript of the trial of the "Chicago Eleven," with bows to *The Investigation,* was full of lights and movement and sound and fury, and while it did, indeed, signify nothing, it nevertheless serves to point up the diversity of production concept that can exist, not only in educational Readers Theatre generally, but even in the same department on the same campus.

A third and especially interesting style of educational Readers Theatre was

From a reading of T. S. Eliot's poetry. This classroom production was done in the simplest possible style, with three reading stools and the readers carrying their texts.

displayed in the 1971 Santa Ana College production of Eugene O'Neill's *The Emperor Jones*. Done with three readers—one for Jones, one for Smithers, and one to read Lem, the soldiers, and the Old Woman—the production utilized some of the traditional Readers Theatre elements, some that are more common to the traditional stage, a variety of hand props and lighting devices, and even some suggestive costuming. The reader at stage left (Smithers) was seated on a reading stool and had a lectern to hold his script. The reader at stage right was squatted cross-legged on the floor, where her low lectern was a stylized log. From this position she not only read but also played the tom-tom called for by the script. Brutus Jones's seat, at stage center, was a stylized tree-stump large enough to hold both Jones and his script, and around which he moved during the chase. Behind the readers was a scrim onto which, during the jungle chase, a leaf pattern was projected. Dancers behind the scrim, in silhouette, provided such effects as "the Little Formless Fears."

Such variety as these productions represent, in spite of the understandably conservative approach to major public performances, argues well for the state of Readers Theatre on the university and college campus. The work is still going on, and new programs are constantly developing in this exciting and fertile field.

CHAPTER 3

Selecting The Literature

The problem of selecting those literary materials which will work best in Readers Theatre is a complex and difficult one, at least partly for the very reason that makes the task artistically and aesthetically rewarding—the enormous abundance of such material. Everything that has ever been written, including original scripts, is available to Readers Theatre, and it does not matter how often any work has been done before, because great literature cannot be worn out. The *Iliad* and *Odyssey* of Homer, in spite of the efforts of the *rhapsodes,* can never be exhausted, any more than can the works of Shakespeare or Milton or Conrad or Eliot. Thus, the selector will find himself surrounded by such a vast bulk of material that he must develop some basic procedures to help in the selection process.

It should be remembered, especially by anyone working in the field of educational Readers Theatre, that an important aspect of selection is *education* itself, i.e., the learning process. The reader-performer broadens himself by reading roles other than those which are best suited to him. In selecting such materials, materials that are to some degree beyond the "ability" of the available performers, the director knows that he may weaken the artistic power of his own production, but he does so gladly in the knowledge that he is giving his student readers an opportunity to grow. This may lead to audience disappointment in some cases, but the director must always remember that, more important than audience satisfaction, there is the educational process going on in his production.

EVALUATING THE AUDIENCE

"Know your audience" is dangerously close to being a cliché, but it contains a basic element of truth. It is probably the most generally ignored cliché in all of theatre. Young people have been bored, frustrated, and even driven into active hostility toward literature and the dramatic experience, and people of all ages have experienced the misery of being forced to sit through a program of ill-considered, badly selected material.

Age level is one of the most important considerations in audience evaluation. While total segregation into adult and juvenile divisions would be quite harmful—such multilevel material as *Alice in Wonderland* or *The Wind in the Willows* can and does appeal to adults and young people alike—it still provides at least a valuable qualification for most performances.

For an audience of children under the age of seven, material that has a strong rhythm and repetitive sequence will be effective, as will fantasy, particularly with five- to seven-year-olds who have reached a point in their development where they not only feel comfortable with witches, ogres, and evil fairies, but revel in the "delicious fear" that these characters arouse. For an audience of from eight to twelve, themes of heroism provide likely material. Fantasy may be suitable, but stories of realistic or historic figures who have attained heroic proportion will perhaps work best. During this period boys and girls tend to divide sharply in their interests, thus the material should contain strong male and female characters if it is to hold both sexes. The early teens is an idealistic age, and if the production is designed for this age group then material dealing with an idealistic search for some truth, or dedication to some worthwhile cause, will be especially effective.

By the late teens adult material should be used. However, even adult audiences can vary greatly. For example, a script designed for the University Women's Club might well be less than a smashing success when delivered before a meeting of the Ladies Farm Circle or the American Association of Business Equipment Manufacturers. Even a general program, designed for an audience in their twenties and thirties, might fail miserably if performed before a general audience in a retirement community. Unlike fifth century Athens or late sixteenth century London, the present-day United States (and to some degree Europe) does not really have a homogeneous audience. There is, certainly, the possibility of reaching a large, general audience through careful selection of broadly based materials, and some Readers Theatre scripts have achieved this objective. However, it is important to remember that the United States particularly, perhaps more than any other country in history, has a variety of audiences, divided by such considerations as age, education, religion, ethnic background, and a myriad of other interests.

THEME AND MOTIF

After audience evaluation, a practical second step toward selecting the literature is reaching a decision regarding theme or motif. In those cases where a particular work or body of literature has already been selected (for example, a production designed to be read before a meeting of the Melville Society), this process is somewhat simplified. What it means, in fact, is finding a spine for the material. To accomplish this there are two possible approaches, theme and motif.

Theme, generally speaking, is an approach that works best in terms of serious, philosophical, literary works; that is, works which tend in some way toward the scholarly. In this sense, theme is the controlling doctrine or thesis that unifies a single work or a collection of works. Such an approach might be used to put together a program of the works of Alexander Pope, using the stated theme of his *Essay on Man:* "Laugh where we must, be candid where we can,/But vindicate the ways of God to man." In the most contemporary sense, theme can also be applied to that abstract quantity or quality embodied in the purely artistic or imaginative work which somehow operates as its controlling force.

The other approach—determination of motif—tends to be especially valuable both in terms of older literature and contemporary literature that has a folk orientation. Motif is a term usually applied to a frequently recurring pattern of character, incident, or concept. These patterns, archetypal in the sense that they exist from the earliest records of man, may be exemplified by the Oedipal motif that explores the dimensions of the mother-son relationship, or the "loathly lady" motif which displays the transmutation of the ugly to the beautiful by way of love and understanding, or any of a number of other such motifs.

Consideration of the potential audience and selection of theme or motif can help to outline boundaries or determine parameters for selecting literature, but it still leaves the director with enormous problems. If all literature is truly available for Readers Theatre production, then "all literature" not only includes the familiar forms, but such things as newspaper and journal articles, radio scripts, television scripts, and to a limited degree even the popular essay.

PLAYS

The director in conventional theatre will almost always choose a play; that is, a work of literature designed for conventional stage production. As Joanna Hawkins Maclay has correctly pointed out, "there is nothing in the definition of theatre . . . that limits it to the presentation of plays."[1] Indeed, such theorists of the conventional stage as Kenneth Tynan and Peter Brook have taken the position that, essentially, anything that happens before an audience and grows out of some kind of artistic impulse, whether in a darkened auditorium, or an empty room, or even on a grassy lawn, is theatre. This attitude undoubtedly contains a kernel of truth, and one might well suggest a debate designed to create a definition of "theatre." However, the theory is usually set aside when Brook or Tynan or any other director is choosing materials for the conventional stage. Rarely do such directors choose novels or short stories or poems: They choose plays because that is the medium in which they are working.

While plays seem to be obviously the best material for traditional theatre, they are not necessarily best for Readers Theatre. They are, of course, the most readily available material since they were written to be performed, with dialogue carefully designed to exclude the necessity of narrative passages. Using such performance-oriented material certainly takes a burden off the shoulders of the Readers Theatre director, relieving him of the responsibility of compiling or otherwise preparing a script, and it does have the added virtue of featuring the literary aspects of a traditional theatre script in a way that a fully acted performance might very well never achieve. "A Readers Theatre treatment of certain plays could provide new insights into the structure or texture of plays that conventional staging might tend to obscure."[2]

However, in spite of the rather obvious appeal of the traditional play as a vehicle for Readers Theatre, the best of such plays are quite regularly staged in conventional theatre. Thus, the most rewarding, valuable, and unique service that Readers Theatre can provide its audiences is not a reworking of conventional drama, but the artistic interpretation of the great literature which is not designed for stage presentation.

From Bram Stoker's *Dracula*. This production used period (though not quite authentic) costumes, full make-up, and suggestive movement to capture the horror that Stoker created in his novel.

LONG, NARRATIVE MATERIALS

In sorting through this huge reservoir of literary material, the first and obvious choice for too many directors is the long and primarily narrative work—either poetry or prose. This is an especially dangerous choice because extensive description or narration tends to become monotonous. However, for the director committed to such a literary work, methods of avoiding the perils inherent in performance of extended narrative materials are discussed in chapter 4. Long poems, such works as Byron's *Don Juan* or *Childe Harold's Pilgrimage,* Shelley's poetic closet drama *Prometheus Unbound,* or Stephen Vincent Benét's *John Brown's Body,* have proved both popular and durable. Related to the long poem, Chaucer's *Canterbury Tales* has often been drawn upon (on at least one occasion in the original late middle English) and Edgar Lee Masters's *Spoon River Anthology* has achieved both a popular and critical success. In the area of the novel the Gothic works like *Dracula* and *Frankenstein* have been particularly successful, along with such highly poetic works as Ray Bradbury's *Dandelion Wine.*

COLLECTIONS OF SHORT MATERIALS

The collection of short materials, while presenting equally great problems in terms of selection and adaptation, is perhaps even more likely for success than the long work. This approach to creating a Readers Theatre script provides several thematic opportunities. The short pieces themselves may be featured, unified in terms of some inherent philosophical or social theme (*... To Meet Mr. Eliot*); or the literary materials may be used in conjunction with diary, journal, or original material to provide an insight into the artist as man (*Dylan*) or the artist as artist (*Brecht on Brecht*). On the other hand, the collection may be designed to feature some inanimate object (*The Golden Gate Bridge*), or a concept or ideal (*The Rivers of America*), where the mere recitation of such names as Shenandoah, Susquehanna, or Swanee, evokes a poetic, emotional response.

MEDIUM LENGTH PROSE WORKS

Medium length prose works, which do not require the cutting that is necessary for the novel, or the joining together that is necessary for shorter materials, provide one of the best, most adaptable mediums for Readers Theatre. The possibilities are almost endless, ranging from serious, poetic works (E. M. Forster's "The Celestial Omnibus"), to realistic-psychological (W. Somerset Maugham's "Lord Mountdrago"), to light but meaningful comedy (James Thurber's "The Secret Life of Walter Mitty"), to stylized realism (Ernest Hemingway's "The Killers").

TELEVISION AND RADIO SCRIPTS

Television and radio scripts must be mentioned here because they are a potential source for some fine Readers Theatre materials; as yet, however, this is a potential that has not been even lightly explored. Partly this is because of the difficulties in getting hold of a script that was probably never published and that is often preserved only in the files of the writer or in the dusty basement storage room of a radio or television station. The work of such great humorists as Fred Allen (especially the "Allen's Alley" scripts) would make first-rate Readers Theatre material, as would cuttings from some of the best of the old radio daytime shows ("Easy Aces"). Some slight effort in this direction has already been made, particularly in the realm of television drama, with productions of such works as James Costigan's *Little Moon of Alban* and Truman Capote's *A Christmas Memory*.

JOURNALISTIC MATERIALS

If all written material is indeed available to Readers Theatre, then two of the most important—and widely ignored—sources are newspapers and journals. Selected carefully and filtered through the artist's judgment and sensitivity, news stories can become the very stuff of art—immediate and yet timeless.

Using journal and newspaper writing, such variants of Readers Theatre as "Living Newspaper" have achieved a limited success as politically or socially oriented guerilla theatre. It may be well to mention at this point a work called *No Excuse*, which was produced by Gil Lazier following what at that time seemed to be the double tragedy of the Kent State shootings and the American invasion of Cambodia. There is no reason to believe that this was great or even memorable drama, at least in terms of any public or critical reaction, but when one reads Lazier's short description of the work's conception and production, the thing that comes through most strongly is the way that this program, made up of a protest poem printed in a newspaper advertisement, newspaper interviews, and other immediate journalistic materials, could so move an audience.[3]

After evaluating the potential audience, determining the general theme or motif, and deciding on the type of literature to be featured, it becomes necessary to determine the specific piece of literature to be used. Coger and White have provided a list of qualities which "should be looked for in any subject matter and style of writing that is being considered for Readers Theatre: *evocative power, compelling characters, action, enriched language,* and *wholeness.*"[4] There can be no quarrel with such a list; the inclusiveness of terms like "evocative power" and "wholeness" make it a difficult one to fault. However, action might well be expanded to "dramatic action," and "wholeness" to "completeness," which is somewhat more descriptive of the concept involved. Also, "descriptive power" should probably be added in the second position on the list. While such an enumeration of specific qualities is undoubtedly valuable, and while such qualities can and must be defined, they are not, in fact, separable. Each, to a large degree, depends on the presence of one or more of the other qualities.

EVOKING AN EMOTIONAL RESPONSE

The material selected should have evocative power; that is, it should have the power to evoke all shades and degrees of emotion. It should be able to make the audience laugh (Kingsley Amis's *Lucky Jim*), or cry (Walt Whitman's "When Lilacs Last in the Dooryard Bloom'd"), chuckle (James Thurber's "The Unicorn in the Garden"), or grieve (F. Scott Fitzgerald's "Babylon Revisited"). In other words, the material should evoke a reasonably specific emotional response, or responses, from the listeners. This evocative power may grow out of the material's expression of some profound philosophical truth (William Humphries's "A Job of the Plains"). It may reflect some aspect of man's relationship to his fellow man (Philip Roth's "Defender of the Faith"); to God (T. S. Eliot's "Four Quartets"); to nature (George R. Stewart's *Storm*); to society (Frank Norris's *Octopus*); or, at its very best, elements of all these qualities (William Faulkner's "The Bear" or Ernest Hemingway's "The Snows of Kilimanjaro").

CREATING A SENSE OF PLACE, PERIOD, OR OBJECT

The material should have descriptive power, which means that it should be capable of creating in the listener, through description, a sense of place or period or object. This is one of the most difficult demands that can be placed on literature, but those works that achieve it are numerous. The sense of place, the re-creation of a specific geographic area, comes through strongly in Washington Irving's description of an autumn trip up the Hudson in "The Legend of Sleepy Hollow," and in a different but equally effective way in Mark Twain's *The Adventures of Huckleberry Finn*. A sense of period can be found in such diverse works as Charles Dickens's *A Tale of Two Cities* and Mary Renault's *The King Must Die*. The sense of object—the imaginative re-creation of some special thing or specific object—can be found in such works as Herman Melville's "Me and My Chimney" and again in *Huckleberry Finn*, where the river itself becomes one of the most important characters in the novel.

STRENGTH OF CHARACTERIZATION

The literature selected should contain characters who strongly interact in the dramatic sense—such characters as Sergeant Croft and Lieutenant Hearn in Norman Mailer's *The Naked and the Dead*, or Captain Flagg and Sergeant Quirt in *What Price Glory*. While this interaction is important and identifies a type of dramatic literature at its very best, it is not always necessary for characters to interact in the traditional sense for characterization to be dramatically powerful. In Eugene O'Neill's *Hughie,* for example, the interaction between Hughie and Erie Smith is subtle and far more complex than it appears on the surface. It is, however, far less important to the structure of the play than is Erie's interaction with his own image of himself. Thus, perhaps more important than person-to-person interaction as a means of achieving dramatic power is the presence of characters who, by providing many-faceted views of themselves, approach what were at a simpler time referred to as fully rounded characters. This means characters who are strongly drawn, clearly defined, and who have depth both vertically and horizontally. Such characters, placed in situations with a high level of conflict, have a meaningful dramatic appeal to the listener.

Another type of characterization, and one which seems on the surface to be almost the direct opposite of the type just discussed, is best exemplified by the works of Charles Dickens. Dickens has often been accused, unjustly in many cases, of creating only flat, one-dimensional characters who are so exaggerated in certain personal characteristics that they become grotesques or caricatures. While one could debate this view in terms of such characters as Pip or Nicholas Nickleby or (perhaps especially) Mr. Pickwick, it is true often enough, in such cases as Uriah Heep, to make a valid point about "compelling characters." In some cases Dickens has indeed created literary caricatures, and it is this very quality—this aspect of being overdrawn or overemphasized—that gives these characters their power, and makes the work of Dickens so attractive for Readers Theatre.

Omitting characterization in any traditional sense is a third possibility. The necessity of having identifiable characters in Readers Theatre is one that is even now being debated, and the possibility of arriving at a final answer seems highly unlikely. Certainly, to do a program concentrating primarily on the poetry of T. S. Eliot or Dylan Thomas or even Shakespeare means that, unless a lot of material is used that stands outside the poetry itself, traditional characterization will not be achieved. In such cases, however, a type of characterization can be achieved in terms of the individual works, in the sense that the poems have an identity of their own in addition to their identity as a part of the total body of the poet's work. Thus, for Eliot, the person reading "The Love Song of J. Alfred Prufrock" would indeed have a different identity than the person reading "Gerontion."

DRAMATIC ACTION

Dramatic action has been defined so many times, in only slightly varying ways, that it seems almost superfluous to redefine it even once more. However, most such definitions have been directed toward literature written specifically for the stage and therefore subject to all the requirements that such a special objective as traditional stage production imposes. On the other hand, dramatic action as it exists in literature not intended for the stage has certain requisites and possibilities of its own, based on greater flexibility of length and certain types of action that are internal to the characters. For such literature the concept of the omniscient author, that creator who knows the dark recesses and hidden byways of a character's mind and soul, and, more importantly, can relate these to an audience, is quite acceptable. Thus, the reader (or listener) can be provided with a character's feelings, thoughts, emotions, and desires to a degree that is impossible for the traditional stage where, even given such traditions as the aside and the soliloquy, these things can at best only be implied in external terms through dialogue and physical action.

However, certain qualities are held in common by nearly all literature, whether intended for stage production or public or private reading, and it is on these qualities that a satisfactory definition of dramatic action may be based. All plots, dramatic or nondramatic, depend upon conflict. In most cases one central character (the *protagonist*) is pitted against an opposing character (the *antagonist*) who seeks to thwart him. The protagonist need not be an individual and may be, in fact, a couple (*Romeo and Juliet*), a family (*The Swiss Family Robinson*), a group of some kind (the union members in *Waiting for Lefty*), or even a nation (some of Shakespeare's historical plays). This is also true of the antagonist, who may be an individual, or a group, or even an opposing force such as "society," represented in so many of the naturalistic novels following the turn of the century. In a work where dramatic action is present, the traditional form calls for the protagonist and antagonist to have a confrontation early in the story, struggle during the middle part of the work, and usually achieve some new form of balance at the conclusion. This new balance generally results from the victory of the protagonist over the antagonist (Dumas's *The Count of Monte Cristo*), but may, upon occasion, take such varying forms as a physical victory by the antagonist and a resulting moral victory by the protagonist (Hemingway's *For Whom the Bell Tolls*). Upon rare occasions new balance is achieved by some form of stalemate out of which grows new understanding (Aeschylus' *Eumenides*).

The fact that a Readers Theatre script is written (or prepared or edited) to be performed before an audience of listeners and, more than some like to credit, viewers, has as much influence on the course of dramatic action as it does on dialogue. The Readers Theatre script must be characterized by compression and objectification. Unlike the novelist, whose only limits are those he (or his publisher) places, the playwright of the traditional theatre must, as Shakespeare said, present his material within "the two-hour's passage of our stage." Even this two-hour's passage is not really available to the Readers Theatre scriptwriter, for in this art form a performance interval of somewhere between an hour and an hour and a quarter is more nearly the rule; this time limit cannot be much exceeded without putting undue strain on the audience's attention and memory.

What all this means is that while the novelist may, for example, retell all of Abraham Lincoln's life, the writer of traditional drama must be more selective, concentrating on some major aspect of that life (perhaps the Lincoln-Douglas Debates), and the composer of a Readers Theatre script must be even more selective, concentrating usually on some single, climactic event (perhaps the Freeport Debate where Lincoln challenged Douglas on the concept of popular sovereignty) or on some strictly limited but meaningful span of time (such as the day or hour of President Lincoln's assassination). In a few cases, such as *In White America,* this concentration is ignored and the script attempts to cover a whole episode, to wrap up hundreds of years of history in one well-chosen package, but such works rarely succeed as drama, even when they succeed as sociology.

RICHNESS OF LANGUAGE

The quality referred to as enriched language is particularly important because, as an art form, Readers Theatre depends on language—on its ability to evoke people and places and things—more than any other artistic endeavor except poetry (which in fact is or can be Readers Theatre). In this sense, certainly, enriched language may be equated with poetic language. This is not to say that only poetry will work well in Readers Theatre. Such a statement would be patently untrue. It is to say, however, that the prose which works best in Readers Theatre is the prose that has a poetic quality, such as Joseph Conrad's "Youth":

> And this is how I see the East. I have seen its secret places and have looked into its very soul; but now I see it always from a small boat, a high outline of mountains, blue and afar in the morning; like faint mist at noon; a jagged wall of purple at sunset. I have the feel of the oar in my hand, the vision of a scorching blue sea in my eyes. And I see a bay, a wide bay, smooth as glass and polished like ice, shimmering in the dark. A red light burns far off upon the gloom of the land, and the night is soft and warm. We drag at the oars with aching arms, and suddenly a puff of wind, a puff faint and tepid and laden with strange odours of blossoms, of aromatic wood, comes out of the still night—the first sigh of the East on my face. That I can never forget. It was impalpable and enslaving, like a charm, like a whispered promise of mysterious delight.[5]

And this poetic quality will usually be present, even when the prose pretends to a kind of hardboiled reality, as in Ernest Hemingway's "Ten Indians":

> After a while he heard his father blow out the lamp and go into his own room. He heard a wind come up in the trees outside and felt it come in cool through the screen. He lay for a long time with his face in the pillow, and after a while he forgot to think about Prudence and finally he went to sleep. When he awoke in the night he heard the wind in the hemlock trees outside the cottage and the waves of the lake coming in on the shore, and he went back to sleep. In the morning there was a big wind blowing and the waves were running high up on the beach and he was awake a long time before he remembered that his heart was broken.[6]

The language of such prose works as these, through the traditional devices of imagery and hyperbole, and such unusual devices (for prose) as alliteration, assonance, and onomatopoeia, manage to create multiple levels of meaning by combining intellectual content with sensory experience. They provide the listener with the fullest possible artistic, aesthetic experience.

UNITY AND COMPLETENESS

Completeness also can serve as a guide to selecting material for Readers Theatre. Whether the material is itself a whole work, or a portion of a longer work, or even a selection of short works, there must be a sense of unity and completeness: a beginning, a middle, and an end. This is hardly a new idea—an idea for which we in our own time can take credit—and in terms of traditional theatre it is at least as old as Aristotle and very probably a good deal older. Aristotle pointed out that a play must be complete, with a beginning, a middle, and an end; and it must have form, with events being ordered in a necessary and probable sequence. It must be neither too short nor too long, so that the audience can grasp both the separate parts and the unity of the whole in a single memory span. The natural limit in size is one that provides a change in the hero's fortunes as a result of proper dramatic causation.

These strictures of Aristotle, set up in terms of the classical Greek drama, also hold true for contemporary Readers Theatre. In fact, they gain in importance because of the necessity for brief (in comparison with the conventional stage) performance and because of the absence of major physical action or spectacle to divert an audience.

EXCERCISES FOR CHAPTER 3

1. Create six potential audiences, such as the American Association of Business Equipment Manufacturers or the East Lynne Garden Club. Evaluate each in terms of controlling interest factors.

2. Identify a literary work that you feel is arranged around a specific theme. Explain the theme and discuss how it unifies the work.

3. Identify a literary work that you feel is arranged around a specific motif. Explain the motif and discuss how it unifies the work.

4. For the first of your potential audiences (see exercise one), select a short, one-act play that you feel might be especially adaptable to the Readers Theatre form. Explain how this particular play is appropriate.

5. Select a long, narrative poem or novel and explain briefly how it is appropriate to your second potential audience.

6. For your third potential audience, prepare a proposed program of short materials that is unified by a specific theme or motif. Explain how this particular program would be appropriate for its intended audience.

7. Select a longer short story or a novella that you feel would adapt well as a program for your fourth audience. Explain its appropriateness.

Excercises For Chapter 3 31

8. For your fifth potential audience, select an appropriate script originally written for the media. (Television and film scripts are often published and are readily available.) How is this selection especially appropriate for its intended audience?

9. Devise an appropriate program of journalistic articles for your sixth potential audience. Clip the articles you intend to use from newspapers or newsweeklies. Explain how this particular program would be appropriate for its intended audience.

10. Find a work of any style or form that you feel contains the following: evocative power, descriptive power, compelling characters, dramatic action, enriched language, and completeness. Explain briefly how each of these qualities is contained in the work you have selected.

11. Check your library for works on poetic form and style. Briefly define the following terms and give an example for each:

         alliteration   hyperbole
         assonance   imagery
         consonance   metaphor
         cacophony   periphrasis
         conceit   onomatopoeia

CHAPTER 4

Adapting The Literature

Having selected the materials along the lines suggested in chapter 3, it now becomes necessary to adapt them to the Readers Theatre form. Adapting literary or even nonliterary materials to this form is a complex process, and one with no hard and fast rules. To a large degree the process depends, in each case, upon the material selected, for the inherent qualities of a literary work tend to determine its physical shape or structure as a theatrical form. Generally speaking, the same process used in selecting the literature holds true for its adaptation: using knowledge of the program and the audience to help mold the final decisions. The amount of time available to present the material will help determine its length; the type of theatre or reading area (proscenium, thrust, classroom, end-staging, etc.) may help to determine how the material is handled, as will the size and make-up of the potential audience. After all, what works well for a small, intimate group in the classroom may fail totally in a large, proscenium-style theatre containing an audience of several hundred.

THE TRADITIONAL PLAY SCRIPT

One of the first choices of Readers Theatre directors looking for material is the traditional stage play and, more recently, the film or television script. Aside from philosophical considerations, there are a number of good and practical reasons for determining to use such a script. Because plays are designed for oral presentation—that is, they present themselves primarily by way of dialogue—they are usually easier to adapt than the more narrative material of, say, the novel. The same holds true for the film or television script, though here the difficulty is compounded because of the extra possibilities inherent in film or tape. In addition to the traditional theatrical conventions, scripts written for film or television use the techniques of cinematography (such as close-up, framing, zoom, or wide angle) in place of or as a supplement to dialogue. Thus, the quick dissolve to a new scene may tell the audience something that makes description of the scene unnecessary, and the close-up of a tearful face can make verbal comment on degree of sorrow superfluous. This can present a real obstacle to the adapter and may require some original writing to overcome these technically caused problems. (In some cases, script changes may be forbidden when permission to stage a play is granted; the contract will specify any limitations.)

Also, traditional plays are sometimes greatly improved by transition to Readers Theatre; the often excessive baggage of set, costume, and staging techniques can get in the way of the literature itself, and when these are stripped away a new and more valid play sometimes emerges. This is particularly true of such plays as *The Persecution and Assassination of Jean-Paul Marat as Performed by the Inmates of the Asylum of Charenton Under the Direction of the Marquis de Sade*. When this work is stripped of the striking visual effects, both setting and make-up, which so often get in the way of the production, it provides a focused, meaningful experience that has something important to say about social values, and, perhaps as importantly, it says these things through fair to good music and better than average dialogue.

The first problem in adapting a full-length play to Readers Theatre is cutting it to an acceptable running time. The average play is between two and two and a half hours. This must, in most cases, be cut to no more than an hour and a quarter. (Concert Theatre productions, it must be noted, often successfully exceed this time limit.) Such cutting is made easier by the fact that most plays have a certain amount of time-consuming, nonverbal action which automatically disappears in the Readers Theatre production. On the other hand, some of this action is so essential to the play that it must be replaced by new dialogue or narrative. Because the play is, in fact, a unified work of literature, there are bound to be some reservations about stringent cutting of scenes and speeches and, on the other hand, about the addition of new scenes or speeches, and to some degree these reservations are justified. For example, is *Hamlet* the same play after the great soliloquies have been shortened and after such scenes as the killing of Polonius and the Gravedigger have been replaced by brief allusions, however well written? Admittedly, *Hamlet* is an extreme example to use in making this point, because it lends itself less to editing than almost any other play, another play from another period might well be cut, and even be a better play because of such cutting. However, the director who feels strongly that such cutting or adding destroys the organic unity of a play, and thus destroys the play itself, should avoid the full-length play entirely and concentrate his efforts on one-act or short two-act plays.

For those directors who feel that plays can, in fact, be altered without loss of organic integrity, some suggestions are in order. Because of their reasonably simple staging, most of the early plays—the Greek, Roman, or Elizabethan—already contain in their dialogue sufficient information to identify time and place and even physical surroundings. Thus, in the *Agamemnon* of Aeschylus, the Watchman not only tells us his physical location, but also the way his body is positioned, the time of day, that he has been on watch for years, and, eventually, his mission:

> WATCHMAN: I pray the gods to quit me of my toils,
> To close the watch I keep, this livelong year;
> For *as a watch-dog lying, not at rest,*
> *Propped on one arm, upon the palace roof*
> *Of Atreus' race,* too long, too well I know
> *The starry conclave of the midnight sky,*
> Too well, the splendours of the firmament,
> The lords of light, whose kingly aspect shows—
> What time they set or climb the sky in turn—
> The year's divisions, bringing frost or fire.
>
> And now, as ever, am *I set to mark*
> When shall stream up the glow of signal-flame,
> The bale-fire bright, and tell its Trojan tale—
> Troy town is ta'en: such issue holds in hope
> She in whose woman's breast beats heart of man.[1]

The Elizabethan plays, like the Greek, because they were written to be staged with a minimal set, usually make evident in their dialogue the physical facts that the listener must know in order to fully visualize the scene. Such material is often referred to as the "sunk" or "implied" stage direction. Thus, in Marlowe's *Edward the Second,* physical action is usually implicit in the lines, with no stage directions present or necessary:

> EDWARD: What? are you moved that Gaveston sits here?
> It is our pleasure; we will have it so
>
> LANCASTER: Your grace doth well to place him by your side,
> For nowhere else the new earl is so safe.[2]

In these four lines we learn that Gaveston is on stage, that he is sitting, where he is sitting, why he is sitting, and the attitudes of both Edward and Lancaster. The inclusion of such material serves not only to advance the action, but to aid the listener's understanding of the play.

Because of this descriptive quality, the early plays often need little except judicious cutting and the provision of appropriate bridges to link the scenes together. On the other hand, the more realistic contemporary plays—plays that depend heavily on stage setting and physical action to make part of their statement—usually require major revisions to fit them to a Readers Theatre format. For example, in Eugene O'Neill's *Long Day's Journey Into Night,* the directions to the actors, when properly performed, are as important as the dialogue in terms of revealing the characters to the audience. In the following passage Mary is speaking to Edmund, but the stage directions for physical action are far more important than the lines she speaks:

> MARY: You mustn't cough like that. It's bad for your throat. You don't want to get a sore throat on top of your cold.
>
> *She kisses him. He stops coughing and gives her a quick apprehensive glance, but if his suspicions are aroused her tenderness makes him renounce them and he believes what he wants to believe for the moment. On the other hand, Jamie knows after one probing look at her that his suspicions* [that she is taking drugs again] *are justified. His eyes fall to stare at the floor, his face sets in an expression of embittered, defensive cynicism. Mary goes on, half sitting on the arm of Edmund's chair, her arm around him, so her face is above and behind his and he cannot look into her eyes.*[3]

Such an extensive direction to the actors is designed to provide the audience with lengthy, nonverbal communication which forwards the action and establishes the characters. Several substantial passages of dialogue would be needed to provide the audience at a Readers Theatre production of the play with the information that such dramatic action would provide an audience at a traditional, fully staged production. A possible solution would be, of course, to have a narrator read the stage directions. However, such extensive narration would soon grow rather tiresome.

For the director who is totally committed to contemporary material, and who wishes to avoid some of the extensive cutting and writing necessary for, say, an O'Neill play like *Long Day's Journey,* the works of the "absurdist" playwrights such as Ionesco or Beckett provide excellent possibilities. In such plays the physical action is often minimal and the action that does exist usually tends toward the symbolic. In Ionesco's "The Lesson," for example, the whole play consists of an essentially "actionless" dialogue between the Professor and the Student. Even when the Professor murders the Student at the end of the play, the murder is done so ritualistically that readers, with only very limited movement, can capture it. The same would hold true for Samuel Beckett's *Waiting for Godot* or even *Endgame.* In addition to the absurdists, such diverse writers as Michel de Ghelderode (*Pantagleize, Barabbas*) and Alfred de Musset (*No Trifling with Love*) have provided short, poetic dramas that are particularly appropriate to Readers Theatre. Even Eugene O'Neill, usually a strong exponent of physical action as a means of performer-audience communication, has provided a marvelously adaptable piece in *Hughie,* where the disintegration of Erie Smith is displayed primarily on a verbal level.

THE RADIO SCRIPT

The radio script is probably the easiest of all materials to adapt to Readers Theatre, for by definition the radio script is designed to be read. These scripts usually make extensive use of a narrator to set the scene, depending on sound effects to provide semirealistic overtones. In recent years serious radio drama has tended to disappear under the onslaught of "Top 10" (or 20 or 40 or 100) type musical programming. However, some of the older shows, that is, shows that existed primarily before the mid-1950's, are the very stuff of Readers Theatre, intermixing individual characters with narration to attain the desired end. The only problem is that such scripts are very hard to locate. Programs such as *First Nighter, Theatre Guild on the Air* (which presented radio adaptations of successful Broadway plays), or the *Molle Mystery Theatre* would be a gold mine for the Readers Theatre director.

PROSE FICTION

Adapting prose fiction can be one of the most demanding and, interestingly enough, one of the most rewarding projects in all of Readers Theatre. There is no "one way" to adapt what are essentially literary materials into a Readers Theatre script. Each selection presents its own special problems and has its own special solutions. However, certain basic steps seem to be common to all such adaptations.

The first step in the process is *carefully* reading and understanding the work that is to be adapted. The fact that the adaptor enjoyed the work when first reading it several years (or even months or weeks) ago might be enough to send him back to the work, determined to adapt it for a Readers Theatre presentation, but it is far from enough to begin the actual process. The adaptor must first *understand* the work, and he must understand it on at least two levels—the emotional and the critical. He must react to the work and then, having assessed the reaction, he must dissect the work to determine what is actually there and how to use it in re-creating in an audience something approaching his own emotional reaction.

One of the primary steps along the way to this realization is determining the point of view. This includes identifying not only the person whose story it is, but the "angle" from which the story is told. There are at least three major variations on point of view. In the first and most common case the author tells the story omnisciently, jumping from character to character, from happening to happening, displaying absolute knowledge of the thoughts, motivations, beliefs, and feelings of all his characters. In most contemporary works this is handled unobtrusively, as in J. J. Marric's (John Creasey) "Gideon of Scotland Yard" series. However, in some earlier works, such as Henry Fielding's *Tom Jones,* the writer is also commentator and introduces himself into the action when he begins, "And now, gentle reader...." A second variation on point of view occurs when the writer delivers his material in the third person, selecting a specific character to act as the writer's "sentient center." This is the character whom the author follows throughout the course of the action, and he gives the reader the thoughts, feelings, and attitudes of that character alone, as Kingsley Amis does for Jim Dixon in *Lucky Jim.* The third major variation on point of view is found in the first-person story; that is, a story told exclusively by one of the characters himself. This character may be the protagonist, as is Frederick Henry in Ernest Hemingway's *A Farewell to Arms,* or primarily an observer of the action, as is Ishmael in Herman Melville's *Moby Dick.* There are other minor variations on point of view, such as the rather unusual second-person type of story, or the variations of James Joyce. But these are rare and easily recognizable, and ground rules must be developed for each individual case.

After reading the work and determining its point of view, the director should select those scenes that will best capture the essence of the work. This is not a major problem in adapting short prose works, but it becomes important when working with the longer short story, and paramount for the novel. Such a selection process can be very difficult because several considerations enter into it. First, there is a real necessity to avoid turning the adaptation into nothing more than a series of highly dramatic scenes. Just as the traditional play "builds," so must the adaptation build to achieve dramatic effect—there must be variety and rhythm in the scenes. This can be achieved by alternating highly dramatic and low-keyed scenes, with each scene rising slightly in level of intensity until the work reaches its climax. This is not to advocate, necessarily, a strict pattern of high-low-high-low; however, some variation in the dramatic level, resulting in the growth of dramatic tension, is essential for a successful production. Second, while excessive description can be tiring to the listener, enough of it must be retained so that the listeners can "see" the production. Descriptive passages may be used to help provide bridges between the scenes selected for inclusion.

Because of its length the short story is probably the most popular type of prose work for adaptation to Readers Theatre. However, the fact that little or no cutting must be done does not automatically eliminate all problems. The short length is, in one sense, a severe handicap in that the adaptor has very few choices; he must work with the *total of the material that is present.* Also, because of its length the short story tends to depend heavily on descriptive detail. Characterization, which in a novel depends on an accretion of knowledge about a character, must in the short story be sketched in briefly but effectively, and often the total effect of the story depends on such description. Thus, a story like "The Seven That Were Hanged," by L. N. Andreyev, will require a great deal of work, for it contains much descriptive material and very little real dialogue. A passage such as the following one about the Minister is important, for it contains material that the audience needs to hear. However, deciding how to handle it is difficult.

> He was afflicted with a kidney trouble. Every violent emotion caused his face, feet, and hands to swell, and made him appear heavier, more massive. Now, like a heap of bloated flesh that made the bed-springs bend, he suffered the anguish of the sick as he felt his face puff up and become, as it were, something foreign to his body. His thoughts recurred obstinately to the cruel fate that his enemies were preparing for him. He evoked one after the other all the horrible attempts of recent date, in which bombs had been thrown against persons as noble as himself and bearing even higher titles, tearing their bodies into a thousand shreds, hurling their brains against foul brick walls, and knocking their teeth from their jaws. And, at these recollections, it seemed to him that his diseased body was another man's body suffering from the fiery shock of the explosion. He pictured to himself his arms detached from his shoulders, his teeth broken, his brain crushed. His legs, stretched out in the bed, grew numb and motionless, the feet pointing upward, like those of a dead man. He breathed noisily, coughing occasionally, to avoid all resemblance to a corpse: he moved about, that he might hear the sound of the metallic springs, the rustling of the silk coverlet. And, to prove that he was really alive, he exclaimed in a loud, clear voice: "Brave fellows! Brave fellows!"[4]

Such a passage may be read by the performer reading the part of the Minister, in which case he can attempt some limited physical representation of those things—physical and spiritual—which beset him. On the other hand it could be given to a narrator who reads while the Minister mimes some of the physical action, reserving only the dialogue ("Brave fellows! Brave fellows!") for the Minister himself. This is a case in which point of view becomes very important. When narrative materials are all given from the point of view of a specific character, then the person reading that character may very well read it. When the narrative material reflects the author's own point of view—the point of view of someone standing outside the action—then it might best be handled by a narrator.

In the short story, where dialogue is plentiful and well written, it is likely to be clipped and rather staccato, for in this form there is little place for the long soliloquy. Hemingway's "Ten Indians" is such a story. It is short, even for a short story; the dialogue is clean and direct and concise; the characterization is clear; and the point of view is not Nick's but the author's. However, even with a story that seems so ideally suited to Readers Theatre techniques, there are problems. A narrator is necessary for several reasons: The physical location of the scenes changes several times and there is no dialogue to indicate these changes; the material that Hemingway provides regarding Nick's thoughts and feelings is given from the point of view of an omniscient and detached observer; and finally, at the end of the story, a paragraph of narrative makes, clearly and poetically, the statement that gives the story point and focus.

The novel, while presenting many of the same problems as the short story, often poses the added hurdle of handling substantially more characters with a limited number of readers. This can confuse the audience as to which of the characters is speaking. This problem has several possible solutions, depending on the material selected. One solution is simply to cut as many of the minor characters as possible without destroying the continuity and effectiveness of the work. Once such cutting has been done, one specific reader may be assigned to each major role, with the minor roles all read by one or two other readers. This solution has the virtue of keeping the major roles clearly delineated and avoids the pitfall of requiring a great deal of name repetition in order to keep the audience constantly advised as to which of the minor characters is speaking. Another potential solution is having a chorus deliver material that, in the novel, is given by one or more of the minor characters. This approach can be particularly effective when dealing with such a poetic novel as Ray Bradbury's *Dandelion Wine*. The last (and probably most common) solution is assigning several minor roles to those readers who are presenting a specific major role. This can be a particularly dangerous solution, requiring great care in assigning such roles; the audience must always be clearly informed when a reader steps out of his major role to read the part of a minor character. Such information can be transmitted by constant referral to proper names, by vocal range and inflection, and even in the way that the reader uses his body.

COLLECTED SHORT WORKS

The preceding material has dealt with methods of adapting single works of sufficient length to provide in themselves complete Readers Theatre programs. However, one of the staples of Readers Theatre is, in fact, the collection of short works assembled around a specific theme or motif. Such programs may draw materials from one source—the works of a specific writer—or from many sources. Besides the short poem, which tends to form the major portion of such programs, the compiler may draw upon essays, diaries, autobiographies, and even newspaper and journal articles. *The Investigation* by Peter Weiss, for example, is made up almost entirely of short selections from the transcripts of the Nuremberg trials.

The set for this reading of Kipling's poetry was composed of 6 x 8 risers arranged to provide several levels, two permanently positioned stools, and a chair that the readers could reposition when necessary.

In creating such a program, the director must surmount the major philosophical obstacle of deciding *exactly* what it is he wants to do. For example, deciding to do a program of the poetry of T. S. Eliot is not one of the last steps, but an early one. Having made such a decision the adapter might well ask himself some rather rhetorical but very important questions: "Is my purpose to feature Eliot's poetry, or do I really wish to feature Eliot *through* his poetry? Do I wish to feature Eliot the poet, or Eliot the man, or do I really wish to feature some philosophical construct that is particularly evident in Eliot's poetry?" After answering these and other pertinent questions, the next step is deciding what particular selection of Eliot's poetry will achieve the end that has been determined. Thus, to capture Eliot's strong religious beliefs one might select materials from "Ash Wednesday" and the "Four Quartets," and even from his poetic dramas, *The Rock* and *Murder in the Cathedral.* To illustrate his feelings about the dead, dry, transitory quality of the contemporary world, which is cluttered with gas-house architecture, sandwich-paper litter, dead rock and dry sand, one might use "The Love Song of J. Alfred Prufrock," "The Hollow Men," the Sweeney poems, and selections from *The Wasteland.* Finally, to capture Eliot the man, one might choose not only selections from the poems, but also from the critical essays. The process of adaptation is, here, a reasonably simple one in that the short poems need no cutting and certainly may not be rewritten. *Thus, the process of selection and adaptation are, in a real sense, one and the same, with the adaptation inherent in the order in which the selections are presented and in the provision of bridges (when necessary) to tie the material together.*

JOURNALISTIC MATERIALS

In terms of adapting the short, nonliterary materials that may be used to construct a Readers Theatre program, the possibilities are endless. Perhaps the best method of illustrating this type of adaptation is to describe such a program, adapted in 1970, and designed to illustrate student dissatisfaction, not merely with the war in Viet Nam, but also with what students considered to be an establishment lack of meaningful moral values. In this production a group of three readers stood, facing the audience, and in recurring sequence read materials taken from the *Los Angeles Times.* The selections themselves alternated between short accounts of battles and even casualty lists, to the ephemeral and usually ridiculous doings of the "jet set" and Hollywood types. This alternation, on a 1-2-1-2 basis, divided between three readers, meant that each reader was provided with selections of a serious nature, as well as the ludicrous materials. The result of this juxtaposition was devastating.

Finally, adaptation, like everything else in Readers Theatre, requires new understandings for each new undertaking. Works of literature are never the same, and even those that seem to be similar on the surface will be, underneath, full of subtle but highly tangible differences. It will be these differences, as much as the similarities, that will determine exactly how the adaptation may be accomplished. Thus the ultimate injunction must be to know the materials thoroughly, on both an emotional and critical level, before beginning this most rewarding of activities.

EXCERCISES FOR CHAPTER 4

1. Adapt the short, one-act play, selected for your potential audience (Exercises for Chapter 3), to Readers Theatre form. Provide a narrator and bridges as needed.

2. Select a single act from a play by Shakespeare or Marlowe and consider the process you would have to follow to adapt it to Readers Theatre.

3. Compare the processes developed for adapting the two selections. How were they similar and how did they differ? Which work required the most new material? Which work required the most expository material?

4. Check your local radio stations and see whether any scripts are still available from shows they might have originated. Check your library for any collections containing radio scripts. If you can locate a script, try reading it aloud to determine the type of alterations, if any, that would have to be made before a public performance in Readers Theatre style.

5. Select a short story and prepare to adapt it to Readers Theatre form. Before you begin developing the adaptation process, make yourself a formal list of such necessary information as mood, setting, point of view, etc. Remember that this is preparation to do an *adaptation;* that the story you select *is* the material and not merely a scenario for a new script.

6. Write out a plan (or scenario) for a program of works by a poet of your choice. Be sure to select one who has a substantial enough body of short poems to provide the program with some variety.

7. Using the theme or motif that you selected in the Exercises for Chapter 3, and the materials you clipped to fulfill the assignment, create a Readers Theatre script of journalistic materials.

8. How do you use juxtaposition for such materials? How do you "build"? What types of bridges, if any, are necessary? Does such a program require exposition?

CHAPTER 5

Creating
The Original Script

All those Readers Theatre scripts that are created or adapted from existing literary materials are, in the broadest sense, "original scripts." However, for the purposes of this chapter, original script is used in its purest sense: not a collection or adaptation of already existing materials, but an original creation. In this sense, the artist who creates an original script for Readers Theatre is as much a playwright as the artist who composes for traditional theatre.

While this book does not pretend to be a complete work on the art of playwriting, a few words must be said on the subject as it specifically applies to Readers Theatre. This becomes necessary because, while there are a number of fine and not-so-fine works that instruct or purport to instruct in the fundamentals of writing the traditional play, there are no works available that deal with the special problems and advantages of writing directly for Readers Theatre. Until very recently almost all the material of Readers Theatre was adapted from existing works, bringing to life the great literary works of all styles and all periods. However, the original script, especially written to be produced in Readers Theatre form, has its own special advantages.

ADVANTAGES AND DISADVANTAGES OF READERS THEATRE

The first thing that the prospective playwright must keep in mind is that Readers Theatre is *not* traditional theatre, and thus certain devices of traditional staging are not available to him. Full makeup and costume is becoming more common, but the fully designed and constructed set, an accepted part of most traditional theatre, is still rather unusual for Readers Theatre. Thus, while the playwright may plan on having costume or makeup or a complete set available to him, having all three at once would be unlikely, and justly so in that it would move his work into the realm of traditional theatre.

Perhaps the major difference between traditional theatre and Readers

Theatre, at least insofar as it affects the playwright, is that Readers Theatre is limited in terms of physical action. This is not to say that performers in Readers Theatre may not move—they can and do in many productions—but such movement is usually closer to symbolic action than to the complete action of the traditional theatre, which is designed primarily to create an illusion of absolute reality.

The fact that Readers Theatre is not traditional theatre, along with forcing on the author certain rather severe restrictions in terms of movement, set, and costume, also provides some unusual freedoms, and these freedoms are fully as important as the restrictions in determining how the writer will approach his work. The first and easily the most important freedom is that Readers Theatre may work extensively with a narrator. Some traditional stage plays have made use of a narrator, such as Thornton Wilder's *Our Town,* where the story is told in episodic fashion by a "Stage Manager" narrator; or Arthur Schnitzler's *Anatol,* where the ubiquitous Max provides a running commentary and sums up what amounts to a series of seven vignettes; or even T. S. Eliot's *Murder in the Cathedral,* where the chorus acts much like a narrator. However, in traditional drama the narrator is unusual; in Readers Theatre it is common enough to be called the rule.

A narrator will provide necessary exposition in a much simpler manner than is needed in traditional theatre, where dialogue must explain past action to the audience. Also, narration may provide a simplified method of scene changing; an excellent example of this is Max's prologue written to introduce a Readers Theatre adaptation of one of the vignettes from Schnitzler's *Anatol:*

> *At rise Max is seated at a small, elegant writing table. He is reading a letter and smoking a long, slim cigar. At first he is totally oblivious of the audience, but after a moment he looks up, discovers them, and addresses them with easy familiarity.*
>
> MAX: Hello. My name is Max, and I'm a friend of Anatol. You haven't met Anatol yet, but he'll be along shortly. I was just reading a letter from him.... (*Looks down at the letter and smiles almost to himself at something it contains.*) It is my task, before Anatol arrives, to set the scene for this little interlude—so, to work. The time is 1893 and the place... Vienna. It is a beautiful city—crowded, bustling, gay.... We hear Mozart in the cafes and waltzes in the grand ballrooms.
>
> *Very delicately, as counterpoint to the rest of Max's speech, we hear the sound of a zither waltz.*
>
> The sidewalks are crowded with people, and the streets with hansom cabs. It is a time of music and laughter, and, above all, it is a time of love... and playing the games of love. It is *la belle epoch*—the beautiful age—and no one is more a part of it than my friend Anatol, and, of course, Bibi....

There is a knock at the door.

(To himself) Here already? *(To audience)* That must be Anatol now. *(Calls out)* Come in.

In such an introduction, by making use of a narrator, we learn something about the place, the time, and the quality of that place and time. We even learn something about the characters themselves, including the narrator, Max, who is also a participant in the action.

A second freedom for the Readers Theatre playwright has to do with the number and type of characters who are available to him. Unlike traditional theatre where, at least in more contemporary times, one actor is required for each role, Readers Theatre performers can do large cast plays with no more than two or three readers. Thus, the handicap that made Eugene O'Neill's *Marco Millions* almost unperformable on a traditional stage (and especially on a professional stage requiring Equity minimum for all players) is of no real concern.

Before the actual writing begins, the Readers Theatre playwright must make several decisions. These cannot easily be listed and treated in a step-by-step manner, for they are interrelated and, in fact, interdependent. A decision in one of these areas must necessarily affect all the other areas under consideration. However, each area should be resolved before the actual script construction begins.

FINDING THE SPINE OF THE PLAY

One of the most important of such decisions is determining the dramatic locus around which the events of the plot may be arranged. Just as for years directors have instructed their players to find the "spine" of the characters they are attempting to bring to life, so must the playwright find the spine of his play. That is, he must find the unifying force, the direction, the theme, or the thread on which his scenic pearls may be strung. This spine is often called the controlling idea, or even the premise, and often it can be summed up in a single phrase. But whatever its name it always has the one major function of providing force and direction to the action—physical or verbal. Thus, in a traditional play such as *Hamlet* it is Hamlet's drive to avenge the wrongs done his father that gives the play impetus and direction. The end result of his revenge will be to heal the wound that the evil actions of men have caused in the society and, indeed, in the body of the country. Every action and speech, in one way or another, aids our understanding of what Hamlet must do, and why it must be done. This is hardly to say that this is all there is to *Hamlet;* great playwrights always provide an enigmatic quality on which audiences of varying times and geographic areas may project their own fears, loves, and desires. However, Hamlet's drive to vengeance certainly is what gives the play its force and direction.

ACTION, CHARACTER, OR PLOT?

Having determined his material and having discovered its spine, the playwright is faced with subsequent decisions that must be made in order to put the material into a workable, artistic form. Should he base his material on physical action, or on plot, which Aristotle implied was primary, or should he attempt to deal with the material through characterization, which Aristotle found to be secondary? This problem, in spite of Aristotle and the common misunderstandings that surround his work, causes the Readers Theatre playwright some real difficulties, for within the boundaries of this form the artist can depend on physical action in only a limited way to display his wares. We have sometimes been told that a traditional play can exist without anything that can be called verbal characterization, but not without some sort of action (such as Beckett's "Act Without Words"). For Readers Theatre this statement might well be reversed; *Readers Theatre, almost of necessity, must place its primary emphasis on verbal characterization.*

The previous discussion has been held within the limited framework of understanding that identifies "dramatic action" as real, physical, onstage action. However, psychological or intellectual action is quite another thing, and fully as valid as physical action. It is on this latter concept that the Readers Theatre playwright must concentrate his efforts. While the player in Readers Theatre may be restricted from physically acting out a play in the traditional sense (and it should be pointed out that some persons seem to feel that such complete action is permissable), there is no prohibition against a theatre of ideas, exemplified traditionally by such plays as Shaw's *Getting Married,* where the physical action is totally subordinated to verbal action and philosophical concept. Also, because Readers Theatre is a form that depends heavily on the imagination and fancy of its audience—on re-creating in the minds of the audience members a time, a place, and even an event—a certain amount of physical action can be implicit in the dialogue, or given to a narrator, and transmitted to the audience in such a way that they are impelled to visualize the physical action.

With a full understanding of the possibilities and limitations of the form, and having resolved the questions of action, character, and spine, the Readers Theatre playwright will then proceed along lines quite similar to those followed by playwrights for the traditional stage. He will develop his own special concepts in terms of plot, theme, character, conflict, and resolution.

Along the way he will consider such attendant problems as orchestration, point of attack, and obligatory scene.

ACTION

By at least one definition, the plot of a play is a system or sequence of actions, and the characters are those persons who, because of the traits of character and disposition with which the author has endowed them, forward and eventually carry out this action. Such a definition is simplistic, however, in the sense that the standard critical vocabulary is not precise enough. On one level, action might be defined as mere physical movement. On a second level, it might be defined as the course of events within the play; that is, the material that the average theatre-goer might provide if asked to summarize what a play was all about. On a third level, the definition of action might be broadened to include the verbal action inherent in the dialogue. On succeeding levels the definition might include symbolic action and psychological action.

The types of action that might be included in such a catalogue and the various combinations in which they might be included are hardly endless, but the possibilities are certainly many. In the same way, the definitions of character may include the speeches made by the specific characters, as well as the speeches made about them; the physical actions of the characters that grow out of their own identifiable personal traits; and even the mannerisms and habits that are so important in giving characters real life on stage.

PLOT

There are any number of possible plots, many of them shaped by the particular dramatic form that is employed. Thus, if the dramatist settles on a form resembling the medieval morality play (because he wishes to support some specific doctrine or dogma) it will impose certain demands on the material itself. In this case it would mean selecting material that is suitable to allegorical presentation and that is divisible into the basic patterns traditional to the morality play. Other dramatic requirements would come into play, depending on whether the writer was determined to use a traditional tragic form, or a comic. But whatever form the writer chooses, and whatever the material, the plot always has as its central purpose the provision of unity of action. This means that the plot has a beginning, a middle, and an end; that it consists of a single, complete, and ordered action in which none of the parts is unnecessary and all are so closely connected—so necessary—

that the removal of any one of them will disrupt the whole. All the action within the plot must be significant action; it must, in some way, forward or advance the plot. It is this very selectivity of incident and event—this ordering of the action—that distinguishes the work of dramatic art from a record, no matter how exact, of the events of real life.

All this is not to say that the potential Readers Theatre dramatist must create only plots based on the strictures of Aristotle. Throughout the centuries such variations on that basic form as the Elizabethan double plot (where a subplot exists for the purposes of counterpoint, explanation, and even comic comment on the main plot) and the "slice-of-life" plot (which purports to record faithfully the flux of life for that period of time when the drama is onstage) have been developed and have proved to be successful. However, because Readers Theatre must depend so completely on the written work without the props of staging and action to fall back on, a closely knit, cohesive plot is highly desirable.

CHARACTER

Like everything else in dramatic literature, whether for traditional theatre or Readers Theatre, character is so closely related to the other elements that it cannot entirely be dissociated from them. Certain general statements, however, can be made with some security. First, a character must be convincing. This is not to say that a character must be real in the sense of realistic theatre; for example, the Professor in Ionesco's "The Lesson" is *real* but not *realistic*. This reality is achieved primarily by making the character consistent in the sense that his actions—physical, intellectual, and verbal—are grounded in that character's clearly demonstrated moral, personal, and social nature.

One of the primary decisions that is usually made about characters in a work of literature, dramatic or nondramatic, is whether they are "flat" or "round." This terminology, by way of E. M. Forster, is simply a shorthand method of identifying those characters who represent "types" and are therefore not presented in great detail, and those fully realized characters who are presented with a wealth of detail and from varying points of view. A round character, in this sense, would be Hamlet and a flat character would be Osric, the courtier. These examples were chosen intentionally from the same play as a graphic illustration of the fact that flat and round characters can comfortably coexist in the same work; in fact, almost every work of dramatic literature includes both types. After all, there is really no reason for Osric, a type character of minor note, to be as fully developed as Hamlet or any other of the main characters in the tragedy. (This does not imply that round characters are always numbered among the major roles and flat characters only exist as minor parts. The reverse is sometimes true. A writer seeking to adapt faithfully one of the Sherlock Holmes stories of Sir Arthur Conan Doyle would be hard put to make Sherlock anything other than the flat character that Doyle originally created, while some minor characters, especially some of the villains, would tend to be round.)

It should be pointed out here, as a caution to performers, that flat and round characters really exist, in theatre, only in a literary sense. Actors and readers regularly go beyond the written word to find the "roundness" of any character they portray. Such "going beyond" is not only the performer's art, it is the performer's duty.

CONFLICT

Conflict, like character, tends to be influenced strongly by other aspects of a dramatic work. For example, conflict must, on one level, be a result of characterization. That is, the major character of a work (the *protagonist*) is pitted against a second major character (the *antagonist*), and the result is dramatic conflict. The object of the conflict is often relatively less important to the audience than the clash between two powerful characters. And there can be numerous variations on characterization. As mentioned in the chapter on adaptation, we can have the group hero as protagonist pitted against a group antagonist, or a protagonist pitted against some elemental force such as storm or earthquake or equivalent natural disaster, or we can have a protagonist pitted against some social force. This last may be a difficult thing for the writer to handle, for in such cases the social force is often of more interest than the characters themselves. This is especially true in such plays as Robert Sherwood's *Idiot's Delight,* where the storm clouds of totalitarianism hanging over Europe are of far more interest than the characters.

In some cases, conflict may almost disappear in the face of intrigue, where the audience is captured less by the basic conflict between the protagonist and antagonist than by the working out of some puzzle. But the conflict is always there, if only in a minimal way. In a courtroom drama the intrigue of the trial may take precedence, but a conflict between the prosecutor and the defender, or between the plaintiff and accused, will always be an important part of the action.

CLIMAX AND RESOLUTION

Once the patterns of plot and character have been resolved, the writer must begin to think in terms of climax and resolution, for these are the ends to which everything else leads. Perhaps the simplest definition of climax is that it is the point of highest interest to the audience. Often used as synonymous with crisis, the climax of a play usually happens at that point in the action when a decisive change must, in the order of things, occur. It has been defined in a number of ways—by the German critic Gustav Freytag as that point where the rising action ends and the falling action begins—but whatever the name or description, the climax must be a logical consequence of the dramatic action that has occurred.

In terms of traditional theatre, perhaps the most common understanding of climax is articulated by Alexander Dean. For Dean, all scenes making up the rising action are minor climaxes, which alternate with transitional scenes or scenes of low emotional intensity, until the major crisis is reached. This crisis propels the action directly to the main climax or obligatory scene.[1] Another term, *denouement* (or unknotting of the plot), is often used in place of resolution, and it is particularly appropriate because this is the point in the work where the action ends, where the mystery is solved, or where the problems are cleared away. In *Romeo and Juliet* this resolution would be the tragic mistakes resulting in the suicides of the title characters and the resultant healing of the breach between their two houses.

"A final word of advice" to potential playwrights often tends toward the superficial, but for the Readers Theatre writer this is not the case, for the final word would have to be *experiment!* Though it is hardly a new form, Readers Theatre, even more than traditional theatre, is still developing. The directions in which it can move, the depths and heights to which it can penetrate, and the paths which it can explore, are all boundless. In the search for the theatre of tomorrow, and the tomorrow after tomorrow, there is no reason why Readers Theatre cannot lead the way.

EXCERCISES FOR CHAPTER 5

1. List the advantages of writing for Readers Theatre rather than for the traditional theatre.

2. List the disadvantages of writing for Readers Theatre rather than for the traditional theatre.

3. Define the "spine" of a work in as many ways as you can. What does it do? Why is it necessary for a writer to find the spine of his play?

4. Using a work of your choice, identify the spine. Explain how and why you came to your conclusion.

5. Define, in your own words and as fully as possible, the following terms:

         action   character
         plot   conflict
         climax   resolution

6. Create a scenario for a Readers Theatre script. Based on your own definitions of the above listed terms, indicate how each will work in your projected script.

CHAPTER 6

Script Analysis

Script analysis—taking a work of literature apart, analyzing the material in each of its several sections, determining the relationships of section to section, and then putting it all back together again and studying it as a total script—is one of the director's primary tasks. To some degree, it is a task that is usually better performed in Readers Theatre than in any other theatrical area because here the director has, more often than not, written or adapted the script and is therefore already closely and critically involved with the material. In most cases it is a collection of poetry that he has examined and assembled with great care, or a story or novel that he has adapted only after painstaking study and research. However, in those cases where an original playscript intended for the traditional stage is to be produced with only minor editing, where a new script written especially for Readers Theatre is to be performed, or where the script was assembled or adapted by someone other than the director, the need for script analysis is every bit as great as it is for the director in traditional theatre. In all forms of interpretation the script is the core of the performance, and if the script is not completely understood by the director then the performance is likely to fail—badly.

Some directors tend to shy away from such detailed analysis, feeling that it is "academic" and must necessarily be dry and boring. Nothing could be less true. Examining the work of art for all of its various truths is every bit as exciting as the search for truth in any field of endeavor. It is heady stuff indeed, and the director who has no interest in pursuing the spiritual, philosophical, and aesthetic truths inherent in his script would be well advised to seek a new profession.

While many of the processes of script analysis have already been covered in the chapters on selecting and adapting materials, something must be said regarding the goal of the *director as director,* and not as selector or adapter. For the director preparing to do a show, the end result of script analysis is interpretation; that is, the interpretation of the work of one artist, by another artist, to an audience. In this sense, interpretation and criticism are one and the same thing, and they can both be reached by the technique of explication—finding out what *exists* in the script, what *happens* in the script, and *why* these things exist and happen.

EXPLICATING THE SCRIPT

Almost every literary critic has his own method of explicating based on his own principles, beliefs, and biases. Certainly there is no one way to approach a literary work. However, certain general steps can be advanced and even listed on some scale of order. One of the first of these steps in explicating a work is determining its meaning in a capsule sense. Lajos Egri refers to this simplified statement of a work's meaning as its "premise." For example, Egri finds the premise of *King Lear* to be "blind trust leads to destruction," and, of *Romeo and Juliet,* "great love defies even death."[1] In many ways this is an unfortunate example of a belief, popular not too many years ago, that each work of art could be summed up in one topic sentence. This belief, now generally out of favor, was succeeded by the concept that Art (always spelled and even vocalized with a capital A) was mysterious and inexplicable—beyond the ken of even the most sensitive critic.

Somewhere between these two extremes, there is a middle ground that can be achieved and that has real value. On one hand, *Romeo and Juliet* is not nearly as simplistic as Egri would have us believe, but on the other hand, it is not inexplicable. Several interlocking premises regarding the play can be derived from the script, and these can legitimately be called the play's *meaning.* For example, on one level Egri is right. This is one play in a long tradition of literary works celebrating the belief that great love does defy even death. On another level, it is Shakespeare's statement that manmade divisions in a country are harmful and can only be healed by the shedding of blood. On a third level, the play makes an ironic statement on the blind fate that seems to rule the affairs of mankind. On still another level, it is a play illustrating the age-old battle between youth and age, in which age learns through the sacrifice of youth. At still another level, the play may be understood, in terms of the deaths of Mercutio, Romeo, and Juliet, as a statement on the evil of violence as a solution to man's problems. Each of these meanings, inseparable, intertwined by the plot and so taken together, provide the complexity that makes this a truly great play.

FINDING THE CONTROLLING IDEA

A next step after determining the general meanings of the work is determining whether those meanings derive in any way from the author's philosophical or sociological concepts. Discovering such controlling ideas or concepts is important in that it not only provides a clearer understanding of the work, but it will help the director in determining where to place the emphasis in his production. Examples of works with strong, controlling ideas or concepts are Ray Bradbury's short story "The Last Martian," or any of the plays of Bertolt Brecht. In the case of *Romeo and Juliet* the philosophical spine of the play is, essentially, Shakespeare's belief in the "great chain of being," which translates into the necessity for the maintenance of a strict personal and social order. Major socio-political wounds in a country or body politic disturb this natural order, and evil is the result of such disturbance. In this case the schism created by the Montagues and Capulets is bad and must be healed through tragic action—the deaths of the young lovers.

DETERMINING THE MOOD

A third step in explication is not only determining the mood (poetic tone, emotional context) of the material, but discovering how this mood is transmitted to the audience. To some degree artists are always craftsmen, with certain tools and techniques at their disposal, and discovering the way they use these tools and techniques will not only tell the director much about the work itself, but will also suggest methods for making the audience aware of the various levels and meanings of the piece. In terms of the literary arts, *words* are the first and foremost tool, and the literary craftsman can use them subtly and to great advantage. T. S. Eliot, for example, in the opening choral ode of his verse drama, *Murder in the Cathedral,* provides a series of death images (sombre, death, darkness, danger, etc.) which totally influence audience perception without ever becoming obtrusive. Edgar Allan Poe, in his essay "The Philosophy of Composition," discusses such techniques, by which a poet transmits an emotional context from the poem to the audience. Poe's technique of carefully selecting each word for its emotional content in order to advance the mood is hardly limited to poetry or poetic drama. Arthur Miller, in *Death of a Salesman,* uses a similar technique to a somewhat different end. Whereas Poe, and to some degree Eliot, were primarily concerned with creating a charged mood or atmosphere, Miller is primarily concerned with telling the audience something about Willy Loman. Thus, in the early scenes of his play the word "lost," or phrases that indicate the quality of "lostness," occur and reoccur. As a result of this repetition the audience knows, early in the play and seemingly intuitively, that Willy is lost in time and space and an ever-burgeoning population. It is the director's job to understand how Miller accomplishes this feat so that line readings can be directed to make the best possible use of what is essentially a technical device employed by the writer.

EXAMINING THE STRUCTURE

After determining the prevailing mood of the work, the director should pay careful attention to formal structure, which relates closely to mood and meaning. The structure of most extended prose works can be illustrated geometrically. That is to say, given a base line that illustrates the beginning and end of a work, the rising action may be traced upward to climax and the descending action traced downward to the end of the work, with the result being a triangle which depicts graphically the outline of the form.[2] In the works of Shakespeare, for example, the climax or high point of the action usually comes near the play's geometrical center; take any play of Shakespeare, count the number of pages, divide by two, and the chances are that you will be close to the climax of the play. Thus, your diagram will be a regular isosceles triangle (△). On the other hand, for French tragedy of the seventeenth and eighteenth centuries the climax is likely to happen early in the play, resulting in a skewed diagram looking like (◿). Such information is valuable to the director because it indicates something about the material of the play itself. French classical tragedy, it can be seen, emphasizes not the material leading up to the tragic action, but the results of the tragic action, and thus the play becomes primarily a lament over what has happened. On the reverse, those works in which the emphasis is on the events leading up to the tragic action may be diagramed as (◺). Again, discovering this pattern indicates to a director how and where to put emphasis. In this latter case, emphasis is obviously on the suspenseful elements of the plot that result in the tragic action.

The Freytagian diagrams illustrated above stand somewhat in opposition to the diagrams in most texts on directing for the traditional theatre. In such directing, where climax is equated to emotional peaks, the script is more regularly diagramed as a series of climaxes, rising ever higher to *the* climax, which usually occurs near the end of the script. The action then falls off swiftly to the denouement: ⌇⌇△. The peak that in the earlier diagram was called climax is, here, called crisis: the point where the action takes a new direction, usually based on a decision made by the protagonist.

Both of these methods for graphically tracing the course of a script are presented, not so the director can choose between them, but so he can see the values of each, for both are essential if the director is to guide his readers in offering the audience the best possible interpretation of the material.

Once the general pattern is discovered, the director will need to analyze the individual scenes to discover how they build and how they contribute to the final denouement. He will have to be alert to such elements as word order and sentence structure within the individual scenes. Once he is aware of the meaning, philosophy, mood, and form, he can proceed to the next step—an analysis of the characters themselves.

CHARACTER ANALYSIS

Character analysis is one of the director's most difficult tasks. It can be shared with the performers, who should be given leeway in developing their own characterizations or interpretations, at least to the degree that they do not conflict with the director's total concept. For the director and the performer alike, character analysis means not only determining any special speech patterns or behavioral characteristics, but also understanding what each character does and why he does it. To achieve this end it may be helpful to use a technique that has attained some popularity with actors in traditional theatre—"scoring" each of the roles. The scores developed by the director need only be minimal when compared to the individual ones developed by each of the performers, but they will be enough to establish character and determine how each of the characters relates to the other characters and to the material as a whole.

There are a number of plans and methods for scoring a role. Essentially, they are all methods designed to enable a performer to totally understand the character he is portraying or interpreting. They provide ways of ascertaining the motivation that inspires everything a specific character says or does. Put simply, scoring a role is merely a matter of completing certain general steps.

Analyze the role to ascertain the character's motivating (overriding or primary) desire. This is always a specific desire which the character can attempt to satisfy through some action, either physical or verbal or both. The motivating desire, when worked out, should always be phrased in a positive way, beginning with "I want to . . ." or "I wish to . . ." and followed by an active verb that expresses the basic desire as clearly as possible. A statement such as "I want to hate John Doe" is not satisfactory because it is not a positive statement regarding a motivating force. In most cases the "hate" is not something the character wants, but merely expresses an emotion that is already present; the motivating desire should be related to satisfying this hatred. Thus, a statement such as "I want to destroy John Doe's image in the community" is far more satisfactory. The first statement is not a statement of want, but an indication of an already existing emotion. The second and more satisfactory comment is a basic desire which would satisfy the existing emotion through the stimulation of *specific action*.

Divide the role into performance units (or beats) that will aid in the accomplishment of the stated desire. Each of these units will have a number of underlying actions which revolve around a motivating intention in terms of the unit. This intention must be directly related not only to those units that come before and after, but also to accomplishment of the motivating desire. Thus, in satisfying the desire to destroy John Doe's image in the community, each unit will be some specific action that is in aid of the stated desire.

DETERMINING THE SUBTEXT

After a general analysis of each character, possibly aided by scoring, the director must carefully examine the material to determine the subtext and to understand the variety of possibilities inherent in the verbal action. One line of dialogue, seemingly quite simple on the surface, will often work toward any number of different ends that are related to the premise of the play and the scores of the roles. For example, in *The Importance of Being Earnest,* Jack Worthing says, "Miss Cardew is the granddaughter of the late Thomas Cardew of 149 Belgrave Square, S.W.; Gervase Park, Dorking, Surrey; and the Sporran, Fifeshire, N.B."[3] On the first level this is merely expositional material that informs Lady Bracknell regarding the family connections and address of Miss Cardew. Underneath this apparently simple statement, however, is another level of meaning which, in the context of the remark, informs Lady Bracknell that Miss Cardew is as wellborn and has family connections (and address) as good as those of Lady Bracknell herself. On a third level, this remark may be taken as a verbal action intended to put Lady Bracknell "in her place."

"HEARING" HOW THE LINES WORK

Finally, and perhaps especially, the director must make himself aware of all the many auditory possibilities inherent in the work which he is about to direct. This means not only how a line must be "read" to achieve the effect the author desired, but also how the line "works." While especially common to poetry, there are a number of devices that are commonly used in prose to accent or heighten a passage. Recognition of such devices and their purpose will help the director determine proper line readings and accents. Reasonably complete studies of poetic and rhetorical devices are generally available and, in fact, can be found in nearly any good handbook on poetic style. Such reading is highly recommended for anyone working in the field of Readers Theatre.

EXERCISES FOR CHAPTER 6

1. Determine the meaning, in a capsule sense, of the play *Elijah,* contained in the last section of this book. What is its premise? What is it "all about?"

2. What is *Elijah's* controlling idea, if any? How does it work within the context of the play?

3. Define the mood of *Elijah*. How is this mood transmitted to the audience, both in terms of the verbal material and the stage directions?

4. Define *Elijah's* structure, both in Freytagian and traditional directorial terms.

5. Score the roles of Elijah and Deus, starting with the motivating (overriding or primary) desire, and following with a specific action for each beat or unit.

6. What is the subtext of *Elijah?*

7. How do the lines of the play "work"? Apply the concepts of figurative language which you defined in the Exercises for Chapter 3.

CHAPTER 7

Casting

The idea persists that casting a Readers Theatre production is, in most ways, like casting a traditional stage production. In reality, while there are some similarities arising from the fact that both are casting processes, the differences are great.

READING MORE THAN ONE ROLE

In traditional theatre, for example, the practice is generally to cast one actor per role, even including the minor roles. There are exceptions to this, of course. Directors casting large shows will often resort to doubling, and sometimes even tripling, in the minor roles. This is especially common with Elizabethan drama, where large casts with many minor roles is the rule rather than the exception. In some instances the reverse is true, and several actors are cast in one role—a recent production of Marlowe's *Dr. Faustus* employed three actors to portray Faustus during the different periods of his life.

However, in over ninety percent of the cases in traditional threatre, a one-to-one ratio of actors to roles is observed. Readers Theatre, because of the types of materials usually offered and the special conditions of performance, is not so tightly bound to convention, and while no figures are available a reasonable guess would be to reverse the percentage, with ten percent of the Readers Theatre shows having a one-to-one ratio and ninety percent having several performers interpreting more than one role.

MALE OR FEMALE?

Readers Theatre is free in ways that go far beyond the possible ratio of actors to roles. Joanna Hawkins Maclay, for example, points with approval to a Readers Theatre production of *Winnie the Pooh,* done with an all-girl cast, which she feels is appropriate in terms of the "universalized" children and animals of A. A. Milne's stories. She also would carry this sexual shift to some of the more traditional theatrical roles, pointing out that a man playing Hedda Gabler "would no doubt tend to underscore Hedda's masculinity, as well as illuminate her latent homosexuality."[1] There is no question that such sex-reversed casting might, at times, provide a new insight into traditional roles. There is also no doubt that the Readers Theatre director has a greater freedom in this regard than the director in traditional theatre. However, traditional theatre productions have long managed such sexual reversal, usually to no point except to satisfy the egos of the performers or directors and to pique the curiosity of the audience. Peg Woffington, as early as the late eighteenth century, made her reputation as an actress playing the male role of Harry Wildair, a dashing and debonair lover, and Sarah Bernhardt became famous for her portrayal of Hamlet. However, though "pants roles" proved successful for some actresses, the equivalent "skirt roles" were avoided by male actors. In recent times, particularly since Genet, such skirt roles have become more common, as illustrated by all-male productions of Edward Albee's *Whos Afraid of Virginia Woolf?* and even of Stephen Sondheim and James Goldman's *Follies*. However, this freedom in traditional theatre is limited quite strictly when compared to the freedom inherent in Readers Theatre.

Before deciding to reverse traditional sexual roles, or even make a major character change, the director must arrive at certain philosophical decisions, or at the very least answer for himself certain leading questions. What is the director's responsibility to the material? Does a novel, for example, as a living work of art in its own form, have any rights when transposed to another medium? Does an audience have rights? When an audience spends its time and money to see a production of *Hedda Gabler*, do they have the right to expect and even demand that Hedda be played by a woman?

Such questions are obviously rhetorical and have no final answers; however, they are valuable to the degree that they provoke thought. At one extreme the director can so enslave himself to the material, the author's presumed intention, and the audience expectation, that he robs himself of all creativity and thus robs his production of the possibility of an imaginative, artistic interpretation. At the other extreme, the director can become so enamored of total artistic freedom, which may be translated into freedom to do exactly as he pleases with no responsibility to anything or anyone other than himself, that he totally destroys his production. In any case, whatever the director decides will have a direct influence on his casting of a production.

PHYSICAL TYPECASTING

In traditional theatre, physical typecasting is especially important because what people see is, for most shows, at least as important as what they hear, and for some shows is even more important. Thus, a plain, unlovely woman probably cannot successfully play Millamant in Congreve's *Way of the World,* no matter how fine an actress she may be; and, on the reverse, it is difficult to imagine a pretty young actress as a Miss Marple, or the female lead in O'Neill's *A Moon for the Misbegotten.* Physical—which is to say, visual—qualities are of great importance to traditional theatre. However, this point may easily be overemphasized and it must be pointed out that actors and actresses often are able to overcome what seem to be major physical handicaps and deliver great performances. Physical typecasting considerations do not, on the whole, apply to Readers Theatre. Some recent types of Readers Theatre have demonstrated an emphasis on the visual aspects of production that move them very close to traditional theatre, but for most productions, the set is still "out front" and the physical qualities of a performer are no more important than the minimal scenic design.

Having said this, it now becomes necessary to add a word of qualification. Just as lawyers have long known that juries cannot totally disregard testimony already given, in spite of judicial instruction that they do so, Readers Theatre directors must remember that audiences cannot totally disregard what they see. Audiences do not view productions of any nature with their eyes closed, and so they must, to some degree, relate what they see with what they hear. For this reason, at least a modest concession to physical type can be valuable in casting.

FACIAL MOBILITY AND BODY RESPONSIVENESS

Far more important than physical type is facial mobility and body responsiveness. While the Readers Theatre performer will never completely "act out" a production, the ability to make the face and body suggest emotion and action is quite important. For example, the well-trained interpreter can, with a mere slump of the shoulders and a drawn face, *suggest* as much about dejection as a traditional theatre actor can *realistically* relate by falling writhing to the floor. This ability to project physically the emotional and intellectual content of the material is one of the primary assets of the performer in Readers Theatre.

VOCAL RANGE AND TONALITY

Probably the major consideration in casting for a medium that emphasizes text—or sound—instead of physical action, is vocal range and tonality. The voice will be the performer's main instrument in transmitting nuances of thought and action, and as such it must be flexible—capable of achieving a variety of patterns. Readers Theatre performers are likely to end up reading several roles in a single production, and thus will be forced to rely heavily on vocal range and pattern to discriminate among these characters. Just as physical types are often cast in traditional theatre because they complement each other visually, so certain voices complement each other aurally, providing either a pleasing pattern of sound, or a spirit-grating dissonance.

Practically speaking, casting for Readers Theatre performances will follow the physical pattern of casting for traditional theatre shows. The starting point, in both cases, will be the tryout where the prospective performer appears before the director and, through a series of readings and/or recitations, demonstrates his interpretive ability. This demonstration may consist of "cold" readings of the material that will eventually be performed, recitations of whatever materials the performer has already committed to memory, or, more recently, carefully conceived improvisations that test the performer's ability, within the general physical limitations of interpretation, to convey emotion through vocal nuance, facial expression, and body attitude.

THE INTERVIEW

A second step in casting is often the interview, where the director can question the performer's experience, desires, and aspirations. The interview can be conducted as a completely separate step, or integrated into the tryout process. For some directors this is the most essential part of casting because, like horse players, they believe that a track record is the only meaningful measure of ability. This attitude, perhaps unfair and certainly not completely accurate, may be acceptable for professional theatre, but it is highly unethical for educational theatre where the director must be at least as concerned with the development of the students as he is with the overall success of the production.

THE CASTING SHEET

Because casting for Readers Theatre means, in many cases, casting a minimum number of performers for a maximum number of roles, a technique sometimes used in traditional theatre may be of special help. This is the "casting sheet," which lists the roles to be cast, the qualities sought, and the probable assignment of roles to specific readers. Following is a sample casting sheet, based on tryouts for a Readers Theatre production of Anouilh's *Mademoiselle Colombe:*

Casting Sheet

MADEMOISELLE COLOMBE

Reader 1

COLOMBE: Young. Pretty. If possible should be capable of capturing an ethereal quality. Begins the play as a seemingly innocent, simple young matron. As she progresses from innocence to worldliness she keeps the innocent facade, but the cracks must begin to show. Facial mobility and body responsiveness need only be average, as she physically holds her facade to the end; the cracks show in her voice. Vocal range should be wide. Prefer a light voice instead of a dark one.

Reader 2

JULIEN: Colombe's husband. Young, handsome, and at most times stern in manner. A militantly pure young man who has rejected the crass values of his mother but who has found nothing with which to replace them except a demanding Puritanism. Facial mobility and body

responsiveness quite important as he
has a broad range of emotional scenes.
Vocal range should be wide to capture
the emotional patterns. The voice should
probably be dark, to play against
Colombe.

Reader 3

MME. ALEXANDRA: No strong physical type, but must be able to portray age. Mme. is an aging but still popular tragic actress. When onstage she is pure ham. Offstage she is a cold, heartless, animal of the theatre, and a practical businesswoman. Facial mobility and body responsiveness should be broad, as should vocal range. When she is "onstage" she is almost the stereotype of the great actress, and when offstage she must have the cold, businesslike manner of a bank examiner.

Reader 4

EDOUARD: Young. Handsome. Julien's brother. He is a charming, immoral man who fully accepts those worldly values which Julien has rejected. Facial mobility and body responsiveness should be at least average; he has few major emotional variations. Vocal range need be no more than average. Prefer a light voice to complement the light personality.

Reader 5

POET-MINE-OWN: No major physical requirements, but must be able to portray age. He is a successful though second-rate poet of the theatre, pompous and opinionated. When not acting the role of the great poet, he is, like Mme. Alexandra, all business. Facial mobility and body responsiveness should be above average. Vocal range should be great. Voice should be dark.

Reader 6

DESCHAMPS: Physically should probably be small to capture the ferret-like quality of this man, who is a bitter, sardonic producer and a real power in the theatre. Facial mobility and body responsiveness need be no more than average, as he tends always to be in character. Vocal range average. Voice may be light or dark.

Reader 7

MME. GEORGES: No major physical requirements. Must be able to portray age. She is Mme. Alexandra's dresser. A solid, elderly woman, whose main concerns in life are the physical ailments of herself and those who are close to her.

GOURGETTE: Mme. Alexandra's secretary. A sardonic, efficient, elderly woman. A bit more human than her employer. Also a bit of an actress herself; she helps Mme. Alexandra in rehearsing lines.

For both roles the facial mobility and body responsiveness must be above average, as they represent two distinct character types. The vocal range must be broad. The voice may be either light or dark, as long as it is flexible.

Reader 8

He must be able to handle several small effeminate male roles on one hand, and a stagehand, physically capable of throwing Julien out of the theatre, on the other.

CHIROPODIST: Small, effeminate male.

MANICURIST: Small, effeminate male.

HAIRDRESSER: Effeminate male.

STAGEHAND: Physically strong male. Must represent a group of stagehands who, near the end of the play, seek to evict Julien from the theatre by force.

GAULOIS: Sophisticated theatrical type and would-be lover of Colombe.

Facial mobility and body responsiveness must be great, to allow this reader to go from the effeminate to the strongly masculine. This is also true of vocal range and effectiveness. The voice may be either light or dark, but prefer a light voice with a strong lower register.

KEEPING ASSIGNMENTS OPEN

After casting has been completed, and performers have been tentatively assigned to roles, a director is well advised to keep the assignments loose for at least the first three days of rehearsal. This might seem a cruel or unusual practice, but it is a common and highly practical one, for the director must watch, during those early rehearsals, to see how the performers mesh in their roles. Shifting may be necessary for any number of reasons, ranging from personal conflicts between performers to judgmental mistakes in casting which result in a performer who is incapable of delivering that quality which seemed to be evident in tryout. If no performer is encouraged to feel that a particular role belongs exclusively to him, such shifting will be easier for the director and less painful to the performer.

EXERCISE FOR CHAPTER 7

1. Using a script that has already been adapted to (or written especially for) the Readers Theatre form, create a casting sheet. This sheet must indicate for each reader:
   a) the total number of specific roles that must be read;
   b) physical type needed;
   c) minimal requirements for facial mobility and body responsiveness;
   d) minimal requirements for vocal range and tonality.

CHAPTER 8

Directing

There are probably as many directing processes and techniques in Readers Theatre as there are directors. The fact that many of these approaches achieve some limited degree of success indicates that there are many valid approaches to directing; there is no one, single method that supercedes all others. The approach finally selected will, to some degree, depend on certain decisions that must be made early, after script evaluation and before beginning the final processes of casting and rehearsal. Such decisions are not, of course, final and may be reevaluated and corrected at any time up to (and in a limited sense, even after) the opening performance. However, such decisions will vitally affect the whole directing process, and for this reason they must be made with great care and only after taking all known factors into account.

Traditionally there are two ways in which an audience receives material from performers on stage: direct address, where the performer speaks directly to the audience, and indirect address, where the fourth wall is removed and the audience "overhears" what happens onstage. There is, however, a third way of providing material to an audience, and that way is, in fact, the essence of Readers Theatre, where there is no pretention to reality, so that the audience is not overhearing what happens onstage. On the other hand, they are not being addressed directly. In this Readers Theatre style of address the lines are delivered to a point in the auditorium, and the audience may then recreate imaginatively the work being read. The director may choose to vary this form of line delivery by having his readers deliver some of their lines to the other readers, and some directly to the audience. In that case, the degree to which the Readers Theatre production *resembles* either direct or indirect address depends primarily on the way in which the director localizes the action.

FOCUS

There are, in fact, three major possibilities for focus in Readers Theatre: The first is "onstage focus," the second is "offstage focus," and the third, which is really a combination of both onstage and offstage focus, may be called "mixed focus."

Onstage focus. The readers look at and respond to each other as characters. There is no attempt to set the scene "out front." This does not mean, however, that the audience is not moved to create the scene imaginatively, filling in the bare stage with a fancied set, and costuming the characters in appropriate garb.

Onstage Focus

Onstage focus means that the action takes place on the stage in front of the audience, with the performers physically aware of and relating in some way to each other. This does not necessarily mean that the performers play to and with each other as they would do in traditional theatre—the degree of movement and staging necessary for such playing would probably be excessive even by the most lenient of Readers Theatre standards. Neither does it mean that the production is designed to convince the audience that what they hear is in fact taking place on stage. What it does mean is that the performers deliver lines directly to each other, and that they are aware of the other characters as physical presences onstage and not merely as entities embodied someplace out front in the mind and fancy of the audience.

Offstage Focus

Offstage focus means, essentially, that the readers onstage are unaware of each other's physical existence on the stage—they react to the

70   Directing

Offstage focus. The lines-of-sight of the two readers intersect at a point midway in the auditorium. In this way the scene is set "out front" in the mind of the audience.

other characters in the script as if those characters existed at some predetermined point out in the auditorium. This is not to say that they are restricted from reacting to the material delivered by another character, but that they react toward that same point to which they deliver their lines. There are a number of possibilities for determining where the performers deliver their lines. They may be delivered directly out toward some point at the back of the auditorium; they may be delivered to a focal point at the center of the auditorium; or, more satisfactorily, they may be delivered in such a manner that they intersect at a point midway out in the center of the auditorium. This intersection works much better than playing directly toward the back wall because it keeps the scene *in* the audience rather than behind it at some infinite, line-of-sight distance. In using such focus it is necessary for the director to make sure that the eyes of all his performers are intersecting at the same point: They are not just speaking to this point in the auditorium, but establishing a scene for both themselves and their audience. It is important that the performers visualize the scene as vividly and in as great a detail as they hope to make the audience see it. In other words, they must interpret it to themselves as well as to the audience; otherwise they are merely readers delivering lines to a roomful of people.

Mixed Focus

The third possibility—mixed focus—is the combination of onstage and offstage focus. This is steadily becoming more popular, for it allows variations to suit any number of situations. The decision to use this mixed form must be based largely on the type of material to be presented. Several potential situations present themselves. First, material containing a number of scene changes can be handled especially well with this method because it provides at least two different scene locations: onstage and out front. Additionally, recent practice has provided at least three out-front playing areas in addition to the stage itself. These offstage playing areas all provide strong reading positions for the performers, and the slight shift in the area of focus aids in imparting to the audience a feeling of physical change in scene location.

The mixed form is also particularly valid for material containing comic scenes, for comedy is almost never a matter of comic line or comic dialogue only, but a combination of these plus timing, and importantly, direct reaction. In other words, in comedy the visual response of a character to what is said can be far more important than what is said. In a recent, student-directed production of *Pierre Pathelin,* the director experimented with those scenes demanding comic reaction, using full reaction in each case, but

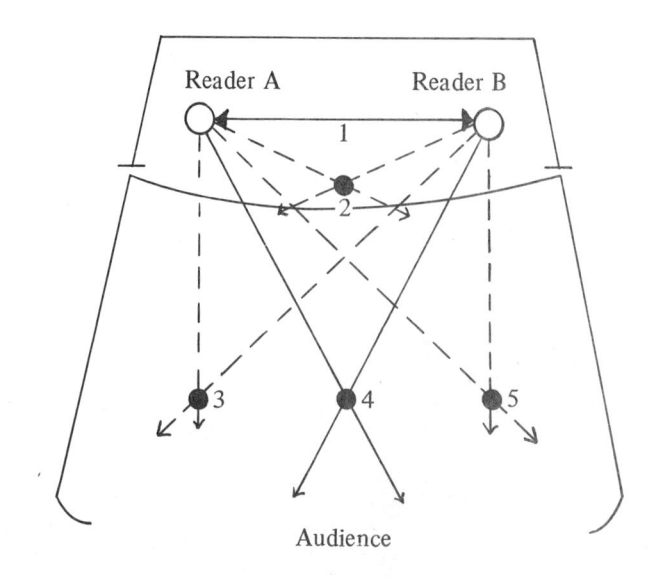

Mixed focus. The five basic points where the scenes may be located using mixed focus—point 1 is onstage focus; point 2 is oblique focus; points 3, 4, and 5 are offstage focus.

working first with offstage focus, and then with two types of onstage focus. The first type of onstage focus was direct contact. The second type was slightly oblique, with the performers turning one quarter down toward the audience, thus keeping the illusion of direct contact but providing slightly stronger reading positions. Of these three types of focus the last proved the most successful in that it provided the effect of direct contact with slightly stronger positioning.

Oblique focus. The lines-of-sight of the two readers intersect at a point close to or even on the stage area.

MOVEMENT

The question of stage movement in Readers Theatre—how much actual, physical movement is acceptable or even allowable—has recently been the subject of great and, upon occasion, acrimonious debate. Readers Theatre deals with several types of movement—suggestive movement, movement as a result of focus, contrasting movement, and limited realistic movement—and it is necessary to know the possibilities of all of these before moving on to a discussion of composition. Thus, certain questions are in order. Is it permissible for performers to actually move, not merely stand up and sit down, but change position on stage? If the answer is affirmative, then how much and in what way may they move without turning Readers Theatre into a poor facsimile of traditional theatre?

Such questions are not easily answered. At one extreme, some traditionalists would like to restrict all movement to sitting and standing. At the other extreme, completely realistic movement is used. For example, at a recent California festival, a production used such complete movement, along with memorized scripts, full costuming, and extensive stage effects, that only the fact that some of the material was narrative separated the production from traditional theatre. Most Readers Theatre productions will fall somewhere between these two extremes.

Coger and White have quite emphatically pointed out that the "arrangement of readers does not have to remain static."[1] It is, in fact, desirable that readers move at least occasionally to avoid a static feeling that even the best reading performance will be hard put to overcome. Sitting and standing provide a variety of visual aspects by changing the pattern, emphasis, and pictorial effect.

The matter of emphasis is always a relative one, and the director must remember that standing is not necessarily a more emphatic position than sitting. On a stage containing three or more seated readers, emphasis can be given any line or passage by having the reader stand during its delivery. On the other hand, equal emphasis can be achieved by the reverse, by keeping the performer who is reading seated, while the silent performers stand. Varying such techniques tends not only to provide the emphasis desired, but also provides an onstage visual interest through variety.

And movement should not necessarily be restricted to sitting and standing. Performers may indeed move about the stage, changing position as their relationships to other characters change. For example, when the script calls for a bit of intense dialogue between two characters, it can be quite damaging to the performance if they are restricted to their original positioning, which may have placed them at opposite ends of the stage grouping. In such a case, the performers should change position so that their dialogue—and the fact that they are confronting each other—is believable. The only danger in such movement is that it can seem quite awkward, as if the director is saying aloud, "Now it's time for the conversation. Readers 1 and 2 must both walk forward to their marks." To avoid such awkward appearing movement, the director should attempt to group his performers in a basic position that takes into account all the possible relationships of the characters onstage, and thus minimizes the necessity for major movements. The idea is to avoid strong moves or crosses that contrast too sharply with the restrained physical quality of the balance of the performance.

Theoretically, the amount of space available for movement on the traditional stage is quite strictly limited: It is bounded by the proscenium arch, or by the edge of the thrust or arena stage. Distance, or space, is also limited by the size of the actor's body in relationship to these constant boundaries and to surrounding stage objects, including the bodies of the other performers.

However, what is true in theory, and indeed in physical fact, can often be surmounted by the artist/performer who, through an act of will, by summoning up all his memories and intelligence, transcends the limits of his physical surroundings and even the limits of his own body.

One of the most influential of recent theorists on space-forming techniques has been Professor Masami Kuni, whose work in terms of dance has been devoted to the forming of what he terms "plus" and "minus" space.[2] For Kuni, space is formed in two ways—physically in contrast to mass, and emotionally-spiritually by the performer "drawing in" to himself and thus creating space around him. Perhaps the best illustration of space-forming by contrast with mass is to visualize a stage containing a group of persons (mass) at stage right, and a single person standing alone at stage left. Physically, the lone performer is surrounded by space, and the degree of space is directly proportional to the size of the stage and the lone performer's distance from the group or mass. The amount of this space, however, can be increased or decreased by the performer's capability of demonstrating isolation.

It must be pointed out that even in terms of the traditional stage, suggested movement is quite common, and so the stage is not bounded by the physical set. This is true even of the proscenium stage, where the set tends on one level to be an enclosing factor. Imagine a proscenium stage containing a set for a classical Greek play, with a large door at stage center which enters the palace, and doors at stage right and left which lead to Athens and Thebes respectively. When a character such as Creon in *Oedipus at Colonos* is dragged away by the soldiers of Theseus, his departure does not necessarily end when he leaves the stage area, depending on the actions and reactions of the characters who remain on stage. They follow after him a few steps, look after him, wave, and otherwise indicate a departing presence on an imagined set that stretches, if not to infinity, at least to Thebes. This is truly suggestive acting in that the performers indicate to the audience a happening which the audience can no longer physically see.

Suggestive Movement

Probably more important to Readers Theatre than actual complete physical movement is suggestive movement, which may be defined as some form of minimal movement that, by way of focus or contrast or some other technique, "suggests" complete movement to the audience. Properly used, suggestive movement can be highly effective.

Movement as a result of focus can be one of the most effective techniques of Readers Theatre in that it allows a dual view of the action. Visualize the scene mentioned previously, from *Oedipus at Colonos,* where Creon is dragged away by the soldiers of Theseus. This time, however, the set is

From Corwin's *The World of Carl Sandburg.* The composition of this scene suggests a dimension beyond the stage area.

minimal: only reading stools and stands. The performers reading the Chorus focus on a point at the rear of the auditorium and, through their attitudes, suggest that they are watching Creon's unwilling departure. Unlike the same scene on the traditional stage, the departing Creon may remain in audience view, rather than disappearing into the wings, suggesting in terms of body stance and expression the misery of a man being dragged away to an unfortunate fate. Thus, the audience sees the scene doubly—seeing the Chorus react to this violent departure, and seeing the reactions of the departing man.

Contrasting movement can also be an effective Readers Theatre device in which the audience sees the speed of movement and also its quality or type in terms of its contrast to some norm. Fast movement by a character gains speed in contrast to someone moving slowly. Such movement can be accomplished in a mime style, with the characters moving in place, or it can be projected by minimal suggestive or even realistic movement. Often the contrast in movement not only takes a character from point A to point B, but also characterizes that person in some way, for audiences relate speed of movement not only to the physical situation, but also to character. The slow character is usually thought of as lethargic on a physical, intellectual, and temperamental basis, and the fast-moving character is thought of as energetic in the same variety of ways.

Limited realistic movement can be very effective in the Readers Theatre form, though it must be used with great care. For example, in a Christmas Eve scene from *Anatol,* by Arthur Schnitzler, Anatol meets a woman and the two walk down a street in Vienna that is crowded with last-minute Christmas shoppers. At first the woman, an ex-mistress of Anatol who has married since their breakup, is brusque and impatient and Anatol is more pursuing her than walking with her. After some dialogue she relents and they walk together and window shop. After a bit more dialogue she becomes the pursuer and, finally, departs reluctantly. In this situation a great deal of actual ground is covered physically, even taking into account the occasional stops for window shopping, and the director's task is to somehow impart this movement to an audience. In realistic or traditional theatre this task is particularly difficult because there is not, literally, room enough on stage to do the scene realistically. However, in the Readers Theatre form the scene can be handled quite effectively, with only spurts of realistic movement on the part of the readers, who face the audience, looking occasionally into shop windows. At first the woman is leading and Anatol following, so that she moves and he is forced to take several fast steps to catch up. At the appropriate point in the script the two move together, and finally Anatol takes the lead. Such realistic movement, often combined with mime techniques, can provide a highly satisfying and meaningful experience for the audience.

COMPOSITION

Having investigated the possibilities for varying types of movement as they apply to Readers Theatre, it is now necessary to move on to one of the most demanding of all tasks, and one of the most satisfying artistically—composition.

Composition (or blocking) has tended to have far more application in traditional theatre than in Readers Theatre, where movement has, at least in the immediate past, been minimal or nonexistent. However, since movement is generally becoming more important in Readers Theatre, the concept of composition—physically shaping the appearance of the stage by careful placement of the performers—is of increasing importance to the Readers Theatre director. Like the older term, "blocking," composition means, essentially, the arrangement of the performers on a three-dimensional set, in a manner that is pleasing to the eye of the beholder. However, composition goes far beyond blocking in that it illuminates the script materials and emphasizes the various performer-to-performer relationships by providing a visual demonstration of the basic physical and psychological relationships. It also supports and enhances the mood of the production.

In its strictest sense, composition does not involve movement at all. Movement—getting performers from one part of the stage to another or, more practically, from their position in one composition to their new position in the next composition—has, to a large extent, already been dealt with. For Readers Theatre (and to some degree for traditional theatre) the best move-

From *Once in a Lifetime*, by George S. Kaufman and Moss Hart. The set featured two chairs, two reading levels, and a cartoon-style backdrop. There is an attempt to *suggest* the 1930s through costuming, without attempting historical accuracy.

ment tends to be the simplest. According to such experts as Francis Hodge, stage composition is, in essence, camera composition, and the director must think in terms of snapshots or stills.[3] The stage picture, like the still photograph, represents caught movement—a moment in time captured and held for its optimum effect. Thus, depending on the length and complexity of the material being presented, a Readers Theatre program will be a series of such compositions, with simple movements marking the end of each composition and introducing the next.

Like everything else within a unified production, the various functions fulfilled by composition are interrelated and, in fact, interdependent. However, for the sake of clarity, they may be discussed separately as long as the areas of interdependence are carefully defined.

Physical and Psychological Relationships

Within the context of a literary work, each character develops a specific physical relationship with the other characters with whom he has even minimum contact, and this relationship can be paralleled and supported by composition. To a large degree this correlates with another function of composition, which is to demonstrate psychological relationships between characters, but the physical relationship is a much broader area and covers even the most incidental relationships—relationships that may have no real psychological basis, but that are dictated by the conditions of the text. For example, an employee will likely stand in a distinct and demonstrable physical relationship to his foreman. This relationship will change in degree but not in kind with his shop superintendent and with the president of his company. It could be argued that the employer-employee relationship is as much a psychological one as it is physical (or economic or social), but in most cases the employee will not have enough personal contact with these people for a valid psychological relationship to develop.

An example of such a relationship can be seen in the Readers Theatre play, *Elijah,* contained in this book. The relationship of Elijah to Deus (God) can clearly be demonstrated through composition—that is, through the relative stage positioning of the two characters. Deus is at all times physically superior to Elijah, not just because he is God, but because Elijah is his servant, his prophet, and so, in a sense, his employee. Thus, whenever Deus and Elijah are onstage together, Deus always takes a position at least one level higher than Elijah. When the play is done with even a minimal set, Deus will always stand at a level above Elijah's head.

Physical relationships can be indicated on a horizontal as well as a vertical basis. In Harold Pinter's *The Homecoming,* Teddy never seems to develop a real psychological relationship with any of the other characters, not even with his own wife. He stands outside, unwilling or unable to participate in the action, not responding emotionally either to his family's animalism or his wife's promiscuity. This intellectual/emotional separation on his part can be illustrated in terms of composition by keeping Teddy physically apart from the other characters when they are onstage. Thus, the visual space that surrounds Teddy parallels and illustrates the spiritual vacuum in which he lives.

Psychological relationships, while far more complex than the essentially physical relationships, may also be illustrated through composition once the basic patterns are understood—that is to say, close psychological attachments can be underscored by physical, onstage closeness, and estrangement can be physicalized by surrounding the estranged character with space. At the end of *The Homecoming,* for example, the final scene has Ruth (Teddy's wife) seated. Joey (Teddy's younger brother) is kneeling with his head in her lap, and Max (Teddy's father) is at her feet, animal-like, on all fours. The closeness of these three characters in their onstage positions depicts quite graphically the close psychological ties that bind them together, and the subservient positions of Joey and Max graphically demonstrate Ruth's domination.

The use of these techniques of composition in producing a Readers Theatre version of Ernest Hemingway's "Hills Like White Elephants," which deals with the breakup of a liaison, could demonstrate the growing estrangement between the man and the woman by gradually increasing the space between them. On the reverse, a developing love affair or friendship could be demonstrated by gradually positioning the readers closer to each other.

Supporting the Mood

Mood, or atmosphere, as it is sometimes called, may be defined as the emotional texture of a script, and the audience must be given that which visually as well as aurally produces a corresponding mood in them. Generally speaking, every work has a dominant, overall mood, though the best works usually include submoods and some complex variations on the dominant mood. These dominant moods can usually be defined in terms of their corresponding emotional content. Thus, moods are tragic or gay, dark or light, foreboding or happy, etc.

Given the emotional variations of mood, much may be done in the area of composition to sustain and even to enhance a work's emotional texture. For example, a production of *The Importance of Being Earnest* demands a mood of lighthearted gaiety, and this can be achieved in terms of space and posture. The readers must be given enough space so that they do not appear to be huddled together, but not so much that isolation or alienation is suggested. A good measure for this is having the characters close enough together so that the audience feels they could touch, if they desired to do so. Posture or physical attitude is also helpful in creating the proper mood, and in this case the readers would adopt light or graceful poses, so the visual emphasis is kept on the upper part of the body and not on the body's gravitational attraction to the earth. When they stand they stretch up, sometimes actually standing on tiptoe, and at other times cocking one foot so that only the toe rests on the floor. When they sit, they sit straight and keep their arms as elevated as possible. Often, while sitting, one foot can be raised to the rung of a reading stool.

Such composition also works in reverse. When the overall mood of a work is sad, the isolation of sorrow can be evoked by widening the space between readers. Their physical attitudes will be dejected and unhappy. Their heads will be held low, their shoulders will be slumped, and their feet will be planted solidly on the floor to emphasize the earthbound quality of sadness.

Other emotional tones can be suggested with the same techniques, once the concept is understood. A production of Bram Stoker's *Dracula,* for example, might have the nonvampire characters huddled up like sheep to indicate fear, and in their physical attitudes they would be hunched down and drawn in to themselves in the presence of the unknown. Dracula himself might stand tall to emphasize his superhuman qualities, and he could be placed in an isolated position where the space surrounding him would emphasize his separation from mankind.

To achieve the fullest possible effect when applying the techniques of composition, the director must know at least the basic principles of graphic composition. Detailed studies of these techniques are, of course, available not only in books on directing for the traditional stage, but in basic works on the graphic arts. Studying the great painters is one way to learn the aesthetics of composition. For the Readers Theatre director, however, there are some added problems not apparent in painting, for the composition must not only be aesthetically pleasing but must also fulfill the demands of the text.

There are eight basic body positions on the proscenium stage, or any form of end staging, and each of these positions has strength in terms of itself and in terms of its relationship to other positions on the stage. By themselves the various strengths of the positions might be rated on a scale of ten points, with ten points the strongest:

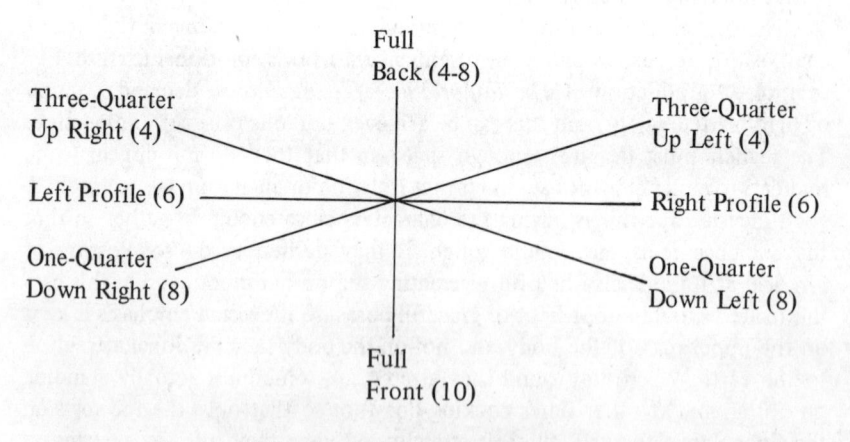

```
                        Full
                      Back (4-8)
                          |
Three-Quarter             |            Three-Quarter
Up Right (4) ╲            |           ╱ Up Left (4)
              ╲           |          ╱
Left Profile (6) ─────────┼───────── Right Profile (6)
              ╱           |          ╲
One-Quarter  ╱            |           ╲ One-Quarter
Down Right (8)            |             Down Left (8)
                          |
                        Full
                      Front (10)
```

STAGE BODY POSITIONS

As evident in the variation of points assigned, the full back position can be very strong or very weak, depending on how it is used. The three-quarter up positions and the full back position have not received much use in Readers Theatre because they create problems in focus and vocal projection. The relative strengths of the basic positions change as two or more performers occupy the same stage, and if they in any way relate to each other on stage these strengths can change even more. Thus, the profile, which is a position of only medium strength, changes to a powerful position when it is used for

Composition 81

The profile is an especially strong stage position when used, as in this case, for the purpose of confrontation. The mass provided by the two readers in close proximity adds to the strength of the position.

In this case the strength of the profile has been weakened several points by the distance between the two readers. The isolation of the characters detracts from their physical response to each other.

The psychological strength of a profile confrontation scene is here reduced by turning the confrontation into a pursuit. The mass created by the proximity of the two readers does help to increase strength, and this strength can be lessened by increasing the space between them.

purposes of confrontation, and this power declines depending on the stage distance between the performers. The relative power of the full profile position can diminish when the profile of one of the performers is reversed, so that the stage composition is no longer one of confrontation, but one of seeking or following. It should be noted that for Readers Theatre the tendency is to play the confrontation scenes in the one-quarter down position instead of the profile, thus allowing two possibilities for focus, one at an intersecting point onstage, and another at an intersecting point in the auditorium.

The Readers Theatre director must keep in mind that composition always has three primary uses. The first and most important is that composition, at the most complex level, provides a means of communicating with the audience in terms of physical and psychological character relationships and attitudes. Second, it supplies a means for enhancing and supporting the mood of the production by paralleling the work's emotional content. And third, it helps in developing a pleasing, aesthetic, visual complement to the spoken material. How these possibilities are utilized by the director depends on his other decisions regarding focus and movement. It also depends on the director's basic beliefs regarding what Readers Theatre really is and what techniques are available to it.

THE SCRIPT

One of the most perplexing problems facing the Readers Theatre director is how to handle the script. If the "readers" are actually reading from the script during the performance, then a certain part of the decision is automatically made—the script must be present onstage and it must be present in a way that allows the readers to make efficient use of it. If, on the other hand, the performers have memorized the script, then the issue becomes whether or not to have the script present at all, and if it is present, to what degree it should be emphasized.

Although there is no really accurate method presently available for measuring such things, the indication is that most Readers Theatre productions, both educational and professional, have the script present and visible onstage. To a large degree this probably reflects the tradition that scripts *must* be present onstage, where the audience can see them and even see the readers using them. This is an understandable tradition—after all, the title *Readers* Theatre implies reading and, hence, a script—and it can be a valuable tradition as well. The visible and useful presence of the text *does* serve to inform the audience that this is a performance of a work of literature, and it *does* remind them that the reader is a performer and not merely the character he is reading.

On the other hand, every year more and more Readers Theatre (Concert Theatre, Story Theatre, etc.) performances are being done without the traditional script. As we have already seen, Readers Theatre scripts are as often memorized as not, and when this is the case the onstage script is merely one more prop that many directors feel can be done away with.

If the performers are, in fact, reading from the script then the script must be onstage and the problem becomes one of handling it so that the readers can use it most effectively. One possibility is the use of traditional lecterns and stools. In this case the script remains on the lectern unless the performers change position or unless the director elects to have them carry their script during some extended movement. This pattern may be varied by having the performers read only while seated before the lecterns, and commit to memory the material necessary to complete any extended movement.

And the actual reading of scripts can as well be accomplished on imaginative, fully furnished sets, sets that go well beyond the simple stools and lecterns. The production of *The Emperor Jones* featured such a set, but the Emperor's throne-chair/stump was cleverly designed to provide a lectern-like area for his script. Even during the jungle sequence, when Jones was moving symbolically around his throne-chair, which had now clearly become a tree stump, the script was in position for him to consult if necessary. The woman playing the tom-tom and reading a number of minor roles was seated on the floor behind a stylized log which held her script. Smithers was seated on a stool, behind a lectern which was antiqued so that it might represent a bar in a south seas island waterfront dive.

If the performers have committed the material to memory, so that the script becomes in effect just one more prop, the director must decide whether to make use of the script at all. If the material is such that there is some value in reminding the audience that this is a reading of a primarily literary work—that is, in putting a block between the viewer and any acceptance of a "theatrical" reality—then the script should probably be present. In most sociological or philosophical works, works in which the *idea* is the key to order, rather than emotional or physical action, the presence of the text will be of real value.

For example, in a production of Brecht's *The Resistible Rise of Arturo Ui* (an attempt to show the rise of Hitler through gangland Chicago) excellent use could be made of the onstage script. It would help to achieve Brecht's concept of alienation (*verfremdungseffekte*) by making the audience constantly aware that this work is not reality but a *theatrical presentation* of a social ill. The script would help in achieving this in much the same way that Brecht's "presentational" acting style helps to remind an audience that what happens in a theatre is not reality; that reality exists *outside* the auditorium. An equivalent use might be made of the onstage script in a production of Dreiser's *An American Tragedy,* where the emphasis is less on the dramatic action than the social criticism inherent in the actions and the eventual execution of Clyde Griffiths.

When the emphasis desired is on the literary work itself, the onstage and visible script can be of great help. This tends to be especially effective in the presentation of classical literature, where the audience reacts not only to the material itself, but to the aura that surrounds the material. Thus a production of Homer's *Iliad* can be enhanced by the presence of the script. In much the same way, a production of "Elijah," based on the Old Testament materials, can be enhanced by the presence onstage not just of a script, but of large, old-appearing volumes of the Old Testament, so that the readers seem to be reading directly from scripture.

Even if the decision is made to have the text present, this does not mean that the performers must necessarily simulate reading. They may do so, pretending to read the whole text, or they may pretend to read parts of the text, delivering other parts from memory, or they may ignore the text, allowing it to remain only an unused visual reminder to the audience.

Whichever decision is made, it must be made to achieve the fullest possible measure of success for the production, and not because of tradition or convention.

Setting

Readers Theatre has, since its renaissance in the early 1950s, tended to ignore full set design as one of the unnecessary trappings of the traditional stage. This is, to a large degree, justified in that the suggestive quality of the performance, depending on vocal nuance rather than complete physical action, could easily be overpowered by an extensive set. Also, since there is no attempt to convince the audience that what exists on stage is real (if only for the duration of the performance), there is no need to try capturing reality with a set. Instead, sets have generally been minimal and suggestive, designed to capture or create a mood. Thus, a white picket fence might suggest the bucolic quality of the old South; a sextant, compass, ship's wheel, and some lines and nets suggest the sea; or a chalkboard and an oak teacher's desk suggest a classroom.

Most Readers Theatre productions are done without even minimal set pieces, making use primarily of dark drapes and raised platforms to provide a variety of reading levels. Some directors use reading stools and lecterns or music stands to hold scripts; others have their performers stand or sit on the raised platforms or on such objects as ladders, boxes, or barrels. In those cases where the script is not employed this can be particularly effective since the performers need not hold the scripts in their hands.

Some recent productions have featured rather elaborate sets, similar in quality to the sets of traditional theatre. The set described in chapter 3 for *The Emperor Jones*, with scrim and props and tree stump, is much closer to the full sets of traditional theatre than to the average Readers Theatre production. There is, of course, no compendium of rules governing set design; however, a word of caution might not be inappropriate. When using a reasonably full, attractive, and provocative set, the visual, onstage qualities of the production are heightened to the degree where they can certainly conflict with offstage focus. Making an audience believe that the action is taking place out front, when they can see a group of performers surrounded by a full set, can create a tension or lack of focus that is destructive to the unity of a production.

Entrances and Exits

The problems of entrances and exits—getting performers on and off stage at the requisite moments—are involved in decisions regarding focus and composition. Unlike traditional theatre, where actors usually enter and

86 Directing

exit realistically, much as they would in an offstage situation, Readers Theatre has tried to keep entrances and exits on an abstract level, involving a mutual agreement between the audience and performers that a person demonstrably present onstage is, in fact, off. Such mutual understandings are common and, in fact, have historical precedent in traditional theatre, as is evidenced by the "aside" and the "soliloquy." However, for Readers Theatre this special agreement can be a real problem because the physical presence of a performer onstage, in any body position, can be quite distracting to an audience.

There are several solutions that have commonly been tried for onstage entrances and exits. Probably the one that has achieved the widest acceptance is having the performer who is exiting lower his head, relax his body, and hold this position for as long as he is offstage. This can be a problem for a performer reading several roles, or for one whose role ends relatively early in the performance. It can also cause a problem for the audience, in terms of their identification of characters, to have a performer assume this offstage position and then immediately come out of it to read a new character or revert to an earlier one.

Another solution to the exit problem has been to have departing performers turn their backs to the audience and remain in this position until they reenter. The trouble with this is the full back can be a powerful stage

The reader on stage right is in the traditional and still common offstage position, with head bowed and arms crossed.

position, and the character whose back is turned, especially when he is in any way referred to by the material being presented, may "take as much stage" as any performer facing the audience.

A third method which has been tried is having the performer "freeze" during the offstage period. This presents problems on two levels. If the freeze posture is in any way visually intriguing or dramatic it may well call too much attention to the "offstage" performer. Also, if the offstage periods are not of short duration, the freeze may well require more physical concentration than the performer is capable of giving.

A final solution, and one that is often impossible to achieve, is using a series of tight, individual spots to illuminate the onstage performers, leaving those offstage in darkness. This solution can only be used when the proper technical equipment is available, and only when the onstage movement is reasonably static—trying realistic movement, for example, illuminated by followspots, would be ludicrous.

The final decision as to which entrance and exit technique to use depends on the material and the earlier directorial decisions. If a decision is made to use reasonably full movement and composition, then realistic entrances and exits are in order. If the decision is to keep all performers in place on stage, then one of the above solutions may be elected, or some combination of these solutions. The guideline must always be the director's decision as to whether the technique is obtrusive. If it gets in the way of the spoken material, if it distracts the audience attention or in any way calls attention to itself, then it is not working properly and should be modified.

Scene Changes

If the director decides to follow one of the more traditional approaches to Readers Theatre staging—that is, working without major sets or set changes and keeping all performers onstage—then he creates for himself a real problem in determining how to handle scene changes or major transitions between elements of the material. How, he must ask himself, can I let the audience know that we have moved from a room in Dunsinane Castle to Birnam Wood, or from Horbury Shrogs near fourteenth-century Wakefield to the fields outside Jerusalem before the birth of Christ? The answer, of course, lies partly in the material itself; without a full set and scene change the script must in some way acquaint the audience with pertinent information about the new locale or the new time period. However, the material may often be profitably aided in some way by visual evidence that there has been a shift in time or place. This can be accomplished by movement and composition—by having the performers change their physical relationships before undertaking the new scene. Another method is having all the performers assume an offstage position for approximately three or more beats. If technical equipment is available, then lighting may be used to shift the scene, with a short blackout followed by a new lighting pattern or special effect. All of these means of transition can be aided by the provision of musical bridges.

The method finally chosen will vary, given the material and the equipment available. What is important is that the director never forget the necessity of correlating the visual and aural elements of the material, so that the audience is given effective visual evidence that one part of the material is over and a new part is about to begin.

Light and Sound

Light and sound can be used with enormous effectiveness in any Readers Theatre presentation. The decisions regarding how and when to use such devices, however, are not so easy to make and again are interrelated with all the other directorial decisions. If reasonably full sets, costume, and movement are to be used, then lighting should also be designed to illuminate, complement, and otherwise enhance the production. However, for more traditional Readers Theatre productions without the full trappings of the traditional stage—which in fact means *most* such productions—lights can often be used in a very special way.

When the equipment is available, tight spots are used to illuminate not only the performer who is speaking, but also those other characters who are onstage and are thus reacting to what is being said. Sometimes, when all performers are onstage and those who exit are doing so by assuming an "offstage attitude," scoops may be used to provide a general level of illumination. The degree of illumination may vary, but it is usually considered essential that the faces of both speakers and listeners be seen clearly. An audience tends to "hear" better when they receive the material in a threefold manner: They hear the words; they watch the words being formed; and they see the effect these words have on the other characters who are immediately concerned. This triple effect is highly important in getting the fullest possible meaning across to an audience.

Upon occasion specials may be used, but care must be taken that these are appropriate to the material and to the rest of the lighting design; that they are not merely used to achieve some startling effect for the sake of spectacle. In a recent production based on the poems of Dylan Thomas, the man reading the role of Dylan was, on one occasion, lit from above and slightly behind with a bright orange gel and, at the same time, from the front with a blue gel. The effect was certainly spectacular, but seemed to remind the audience too much of a color television set badly out of adjustment. Later, however, breaking all the rules that require the reader's face to be clearly lit, the same reader stood in shadow outline behind an empty rocking chair that was lit with a soft blue gel and read "Do Not Go Gentle Into That Good Night." The effect was electrifying.

While the use of special lighting is not always possible, especially for those shows designed for classroom presentation or for touring, music and a variety of sound effects are always available at no more than the cost of a good tape recorder. These can be quite effective in creating and supporting a mood, and in providing bridges at transitional points. In addition to "mechanical" sound, live music and sound are also popular. A number of choral musical sounds have been employed in Readers Theatre productions, such as humming and wordless musical sequences. Onstage performers have also produced such sound effects as vocal dissonance, crowd noises, and even animal and mechanical sounds. Also, traditional songs with such onstage musical accompaniment as the guitar and harmonica have been used with real success.

The primary considerations regarding the use of background sound effects are whether they effectively complement the spoken material or whether they in any way interfere with it. For example, the background noises so necessary for Elmer Rice's *Street Scene* would merely be distracting in a production of *USA,* and the tom-tom which beats all through *The Emperor Jones* would be valid only in short segments of a production of Conrad's *Heart of Darkness.* If such background sounds are judged necessary, then they must be produced at a level that does not interfere with the words of the script, for the emphasis in Readers Theatre must always be on the material and not on technical tricks.

There is some feeling that popular or well-known music tends to call too much attention to itself, thereby distracting attention from the literary material. This is undoubtedly true, if the music is used indiscriminately, for music has an enormous evocative power of its own. However, *The World of Carl Sandburg* benefits greatly from Sandburg's own interest in American folk music, and a program on the rivers of America could make excellent use of such musical works as "Shenandoah" and "Beautiful Ohio."

Costuming

There are no hard and fast rules regarding costuming for the Readers Theatre stage. Certainly costuming can be a helpful and, in some cases, essential part of any Readers Theatre production. The proper costumes can help to set a scene by identifying a time and place far more effectively than a page of expository dialogue or narration. On the other hand, like the complete set, the use of full costume can work against offstage focus, making the audience so aware of the performers onstage that they cannot successfully locate the scene out front.

The tendency, following the success of *Don Juan in Hell,* was to dress all performers in evening dress. This worked well for *Don Juan* and continues to work for any material similar in tone, for it sets the readers apart from the audience and identifies them as performers in a program of highly sophisticated material. However, what worked well for *Don Juan* seemed somehow inappropriate for such a work as *Spoon River Anthology.* Also, the performers in *Spoon River* read multiple roles (those in *Don Juan* did not) and had to indicate their new characters through their costumes. This kind of situation gave birth to second primary type of Readers Theatre costuming—a simple costume that appears basically appropriate to the time and place and situation (though not necessarily historically accurate) and that is capable of suggesting a variety of characters through changing such minimal items as hats, scarves, and neckerchiefs.

In educational Readers Theatre, this last style of costuming seems to have achieved widespread acceptance. However, in many cases the departmental or school budget dictates doing shows in contemporary street dress, and though often less satisfactory, this can work very well indeed. Neat, reasonably dressy and unobtrusive street clothing can work well for historical material as well as contemporary. In part this is because the familiarity the audience has with current fashions leads them to discount the clothing completely. This discounting of costume can be valuable to the Readers Theatre production because it lends strength to the offstage action that takes place in the mind of the audience.

These, then, are the primary areas that must be considered in directing the Readers Theatre production. There is no established order or sequence for dealing with these areas; they are all interlocking and, in fact, interdependent. Once the decisions are made and carefully considered in terms of their interrelated effect, the director has taken an important step in achieving a unified, organically whole production.

EXERCISES FOR CHAPTER 8

1. Using diagrams (based on the Stage Body Positions diagram in this chapter) illustrate all the potentials for focus, including onstage, offstage, and mixed.

2. Alternating as director and performer, experiment with space forming techniques. Create isolation in contrast with mass, and create isolation by helping the reader to draw in to himself.

Exercises 3 through 9 are based on the one-act play Headaches, Heartaches, and Innocence Be Damned, *contained in this book.*

Exercises For Chapter 8   91

3. Assuming a reading (staging) area of 25' x 20', create a groundplan for the play. You may furnish your area with three (or less) adjustable risers, lecterns and stools, and with no more than three simple set pieces, such as tables and chairs.

4. Determine the reader positioning (blocking) for each of the "still" compositions that you find to be necessary in illuminating the script. Write a brief explanation of how you arrived at each specific composition. (Include concepts of physical and psychological relationship and mood.) Indicate these positions on copies of your groundplan.

5. Indicate on copies of your groundplan the movement necessary to get your readers from their positions in each still composition to their positions in the next composition. Discuss briefly the type or quality of the movement and indicate why you elected to use it.

6. Using your groundplan, create a lighting plot for your production. It need not be highly technical, but indicate the type of lighting effect desired, the intensity, and any specials that might be required.

7. Discuss briefly any audio requirements, beyond the voices of the readers, necessary to the production. Consider pre-show, entre act, bridges, etc.

8. Indicate through sketches and/or description the type of costuming you envision and indicate why you arrived at this choice.

9. Discuss any other aspects of the show that need special attention, such as scripts, entrances and exits, etc.

CHAPTER 9

Rehearsals And Performance

Most rehearsal periods break down into basically similar units: early rehearsals designed to acquaint performers with total concepts and characterizations; middle rehearsals which take up the largest portion of time because this is where performers work out the problems of their roles; and final rehearsals which provide a renewed sense of continuity for both performers and director and allow for necessary technical practice. These units tend to follow similar patterns no matter what the directorial technique. The various processes that take place and the decisions that are made during this lengthy rehearsal period (in educational theatre usually from four to six weeks) are many and varied, depending on both the director and his cast.

EARLY REHEARSALS

After casting has been completed and roles assigned, it is standard procedure to call everyone together to hold a series of early, read-through rehearsals. These should not be considered an extension of tryouts, though the director would be well advised to let his performers know that selections are still tentative and subject to revision should his early judgment prove faulty.

The first read-through can be very important for the director and the performer alike, and there are several ways of handling this gathering. Some directors like to read the script, entirely by themselves, to the listening cast. This gives the performers a real feeling (through demonstration) for the directorial concept, and it does provide the underprivileged director with an opportunity to star, however briefly or faintly. However, unless the director is a highly skillful reader, capable of doing complete justice to all the roles—male and female, young and old—then the dangers far outweigh the advantages. At best such directorial readings tend to be unfruitful; at worst they can be quite harmful. If the director is a good reader then his reading will possibly become something that the performers seek, perhaps consciously and perhaps subconsciously, to imitate, and this will almost surely cause a flatness or sameness in the level of all performances, with all the performers sounding just a bit alike. Also, there is a danger that the line readings of the director, his inflections and intonations, will badly mislead some of the performers, conflicting with their own valid interpretations.

Probably the most successful way to handle the first read-through is for the director to present a brief concept of the whole script, giving the performers an idea of the aim of the total production. There is little point in specifically explaining what is wanted from each role before the performers have a chance to demonstrate what they are capable of giving. Such specifics tend to cripple the creativity of the individual interpreter, thereby robbing the performance of the richness that group interpretation should provide. If desired the director can follow his remarks on the total concept with a factual presentation of production designs, ground plans, models or elevations of settings (if any), and some discussion of such basic problems as use of scripts, degree of composition, and amount of movement that will be employed. All of this, however, should be kept to a minimum because, at that first meeting, the main thing that all the performers are anxious to do is to read their role or roles aloud—to give voice to the script.

The most important thing that the director will give his performers in this first session is an indication of direction or aim, and just enough material on characterization for each role so that none of the performers ends up developing characters who fail to fit into the total concept. Also, if the script is an adaptation or cutting of a literary work, or a compilation of several literary works, the director should end the session with the admonition that each performer immediately read the original, taking notes either on paper or mentally, of ideas for characterization.

Following this first read-through there will be a number of rehearsal sessions "around the table," reading and discussing and analyzing the script. There is no real uniformity of opinion regarding how much time should be devoted to this process. Some directors go from the first read-through rehearsal directly into the middle rehearsals; other equally successful directors will spend up to two weeks around the table. The decision as to when to end the early rehearsals will depend on the varying temperaments of the director and his cast, and also on the complexity of the material being read.

The primary purpose of these early rehearsals is to allow each performer a sense of total characterization which the middle rehearsal period—broken into small, rehearsable units—does not allow. Thus, while they are still working with the total script, the performers should be encouraged not to stylize or characterize too fully, but to concentrate on understanding their total character and its relationship to all the other characters and events of the script. When any one character is examined in terms of all the possible relationships, whole new patterns of understanding open up, and if stylized, expressive readings are developed too early they may prove to be wrong and very difficult to correct at some later stage of rehearsal.

One of the main things for both the director and performer to look for in this early stage of rehearsal is character consistency. Where is the character at each step along the way? Where does he end up? Does he change? If so, how much, in what way, and as a result of what business or relationship? This sort of questioning and exploration cannot really be accomplished in the middle rehearsals, where emphasis will be on perfecting scenes or units of the script, and technical or dress rehearsals will be too late. If these early rehearsals are used properly—to explore the material and determine character development and relationships—they will not only aid in making the middle rehearsals go well and profitably, they will also assure that, when the whole script is put back together at final read-throughs, there will be a consistency, a unity, an organic quality to the whole production.

MIDDLE REHEARSALS

At the point where the fullest possible value has been wrung from the complete read-throughs, explorations, and debates of the early rehearsals, the director will move his cast into the specifics of the middle rehearsals. Usually these rehearsals, unless the intended production is brief, are of easily handled scenes or units within the script. This allows the performers to concentrate on the problems inherent in each unit, and to resolve them before moving on to the next. It is the director's responsibility to determine these units, using as his guide the basic structure of the script itself. They should be short enough in length to be handled comfortably in a single rehearsal period, and they should have within them some unifying principle. This may be based on physical action (an event that has boundaries based on geography, time, or physical action) or emotional action (an emotional pattern followed to its climax), or it may be based simply on quantity of material (as in a script that is primarily a collection of poetry).

This middle period, usually the longest of the three-part rehearsal sequence, is when the director and cast begin applying those insights gained in the early rehearsals. Also, they begin the practical hard work of putting a performance together. This is not to say that the performers do not continue to grow during these rehearsals, that exploration and debate is completely ended and they stop short at the insights and basic ideas gained during the early read-throughs and discussions. In fact, the opposite is usually true, and as the middle rehearsals proceed and the performers get deeper into their characters, they will, with the director's encouragement and help, discover depths beyond the early, shallow readings. In part this is a result of the intense concentration that these rehearsals require, and in part it is a result of the exchange that takes place among the various characters being portrayed.

This exchange is a natural outgrowth of the rehearsal situation, and because of the possibilities it provides for in depth understanding it should be strongly encouraged by the director. What it consists of, basically, is a type of critical interplay where each character who responds to a line, either vocally or visually or both, not only gives the line part of its meaning through his response, but often provides some important information on the delivery of the next line. Thus, by studying the reactions of his fellow readers the individual performer not only gains insight into the line he has just delivered, but often into the line that he will deliver next.

At the beginning of rehearsal for each scene or unit the director should acquaint the performers with the scenic composition he plans to use: In the terminology of traditional theatre, he should block the scene. Some directors prefer to have a complete blocking rehearsal between the early and middle rehearsals, so that when the unit begins rehearsal the performers already know their physical movements, either those that they will personally perform onstage, or those that have been described for them in terms of the scene out front. This can work well for Readers Theatre, with its generally limited degree of movement. However, as composition and movement become more complex, the amount a performer must learn becomes too great to be imparted in one or two sessions, and so most directors tend to block each unit as it comes up. Early "paper" composition by the director, or moving buttons (or chess pawns) about on a scale model of the set, will help to make this go swiftly and well.

Even in those cases where the performers remain seated, or at least placed, in essentially the same position for the major part of the production, it is important that the director block scenes for them out front. This helps the performers to visualize the scene, to "see" it imaginatively in the same way that they wish the audience to see it, and it assures that all performers will see the scene in a similar way. Also, it will help in changing the scene, in making sure that all lines are delivered to a character in an existing scene at a specific point in the auditorium, and not just delivered to someplace out front.

When a director rehearses an individual performer he functions both as director and as coach, and thus he has two equally important objectives—to help the performer gain the fullest, most complete understanding of his role, and to guide him in arriving at the best technical method of objectifying that understanding for an audience. How the director does this will depend on the specific performer, the type of script, and his own directorial concept of the performance.

In addition to providing coaching for the individual performer, the director must worry about group performance, seeking to assure that all the roles complement each other and that the whole cast is working toward a common goal or end. Also, as part of this process, the director must develop pace or tempo, not just for individual characters, but for the whole production. While this is, to some degree, a part of the performing process and determined by the material itself, it is ultimately the director's task to set the pace. This can be a problem because some characters may be swift or slow in thought, movement, or vocal delivery. Also, the performers, with their own physical capabilities, will often drag down or speed up the pace beyond the rate desired. In such cases the director must, through coaching, counting, or any other available technique, help that performer to exceed his own metabolism and follow a tempo commensurate with the total objective of the performance.

One of the hurdles standing in the way of achieving proper tempo, focus, and even projection, is that Readers Theatre, by its very nature, may demand either reading or looking at the script on stage. This means that the performer is looking down, away from the audience. If this looking down is brief it presents no problem and can even make the performance more effective by calling audience attention to the script. If, however, the performer is too dependent on the script, it can pose real problems. It not only hinders vocal projection, it prevents the performer from achieving fully *visible* facial mobility. This is especially damaging, for when the audience cannot see the words being formed, or a performer's facial reaction to words spoken by himself or by the other characters onstage, it inhibits their ability to "hear" and visualize the material. In such cases, the director must help the performer free his eyes from the attraction of the page.

In recent years, especially in traditional theatre, the "warming up" or "freeing" exercise prior to rehearsal and performance has become increasingly popular with performers and directors alike. Just as a pitcher warms up his throwing arm in the bullpen, or a singer loosens his voice by doing scales, or a dancer stretches his muscles through exercise, so the theatrical performer may feel the need for such a warming-up device. The degree to which such exercises are necessary is open to question, but Readers Theatre performers doing demanding vocal roles may want, and in fact need, the same type of vocal loosening used by singers. Also, some performers feel that such exercises, especially physical exercises, help them get rid of excess tension, emotional stress, and inhibitions brought into the theatre from the outside. There is no intention here to either encourage or discourage such devices. If the cast feels they are necessary, the director should allot time for them.

In the pressure of coaching individual performers and worrying about the separate units or scenes, it is all too easy to forget that the primary concern must always be with directing the ensemble. A large part of the director's task is assuring that there will be *one* performance in terms of concept and stylistic consistency. This can be achieved by stressing, from beginning to end, sureness of movement, economy of gesture, and authority in each performer's delivery of lines. If these are all captured, the audience will feel that the cast knows exactly what it wants to do and, importantly, just how to do it.

One of the special problems in Readers Theatre is the handling of choral passages. These exist as well, of course, in traditional theatre scripts (in the classic Greek plays and in such modern works as T. S. Eliot's *Murder in the Cathedral*), but they could hardly be considered common. However, what is uncommon for traditional theatre often is common in Readers Theatre, and handling such choral passages can prove to be a major stumbling block for the tyro director.

There are basically three ways to handle a chorus or choral passage. The first is historical in the sense that the chorus is treated much as it was in the early Greek pre-Christian drama. The second is much more contemporary and individualistic, allowing the chorus members to retain much of their individuality. The third is primarily musical in nature, with the chorus treated like a glee club or choir.

The historical method of handling the chorus emphasizes the ritualistic nature of choral response by eliminating all naturalistic elements. The chorus is treated as a single unit, with all its members responding in unison, moving together, gesturing together, and speaking together. When practical—when the chorus exists as a separately cast entity and not a collection of otherwise individualized characters in the script—the chorus members may even be dressed alike and made up alike. While this method can be quite effective in terms of ritual, it does have the major disadvantage of not allowing for visual or vocal variation. In any script containing a large amount of choral material, it can lead to a somewhat flat, uninteresting, and monotonous performance.

The second, more realistic method, is to consider each member of the chorus as an individual, assigning lines as they seem appropriate to the special characters, and allowing these characters to move and gesture in a realistic style and in accordance with the personality of the role. This method provides a variety of visual and vocal interest, and its only major disadvantage is that the choral effect may be lost. Also, if the chorus is composed of a group of onstage characters, this method may confuse the audience by making it difficult to differentiate between the character and the choral member.

The third and in many ways most effective method of handling the chorus is to think of it as a choir, with the Readers Theatre director functioning as musical director and thinking in musical terms. The chorus may then be divided into sections on the basis of vocal range and quality, with tenors, basses, altos, and sopranos. The choral passages can then be broken down and the various passages assigned to appropriate musical sections. Thus, the heavy or portentous passages may be assigned to the basses and altos, with the lighter material handled by the tenors and sopranos. This method also allows for such variations as solos and duets, and for the dark voices to be used against the light voices to produce antiphonal effects.

FINAL REHEARSALS

Approximately five days before performance, the cast will suspend their work on scenes and units and move into the final rehearsal phase. Exactly how many days these final rehearsals will take is problematical, depending primarily on the technical difficulty of the show. A reasonable pattern, assuming a show with costume other than street dress and some music and lights, would be one day devoted to costume, two days devoted to technical rehearsals, and two days devoted to complete dress rehearsals.

The period of final reheasals should begin with a costume parade. The actors, in costume but without makeup (it might soil the costumes), should first appear singly and then, as a company, move through their blocking. This allows the director to examine each costume as it appears on the character, both individually and in relation to the other costumes. There will be very few changes made at this time, since the director will already have seen and approved the costume designs. Primarily this period provides the performers with a chance to move about in the costumes and learn to cope with any special problems, such as sitting in a hoop skirt or handling a full cape. Even if the production calls for street clothes, the parade should be held with those specific clothes to make sure that there are no unfortunate choices of color or style. This will take very little time, should pose no special problems, and may be followed by a read-through of the whole script.

The next two rehearsal periods should be given over to technical rehearsals—that is, lights and sound. The first of these will require little on the part of the performers except that they be present in costume to walk through their blocking. Ideally, in a professional production, this would be handled by stand-ins; however, in educational theatre this is rarely possible. The purpose of the first technical rehearsal is to give the stage technicians and crew the opportunity to practice their assignments, run through cues, and make the technical adjustments that are always necessary, such as focusing and setting levels on the lighting instruments and getting rid of hot spots and shadow areas. For a fully staged production this rehearsal is usually a long and difficult session. However, in those Readers Theatre productions where lighting and sound effects are few, it may take very little time and can be followed by a read-through.

The second technical rehearsal is normally a complete run-through of the show, allowing the technicians and crew an opportunity to practice their cues in an orderly sequence, with timing close to what it will be in dress rehearsal and production. The purpose of this is final coordination of all the technical elements of the show, and thus all set pieces, furniture, props, and costumes that will be used in the final production should be onstage and in place. The director should make no attempt to use this as a dress rehearsal, for seldom will the show run straight through. In fact, those long passages where there is no change of lights or scenery and no use of sound may be skipped to allow the technicians to get through their cues, and to allow the performers to get used to handling props, timing entrances and exits, and adjusting to the lights.

The last two rehearsals should be dress rehearsals, which means running the show in the same way that it will be presented before an audience. If the director has taken the proper precautions and not postponed anything until the last moment, these rehearsals should go straight through and reasonably well. However, it will be the cast's first time in makeup, and so some adjustments may have to be made either before or after the run-through begins. The director should explain to the cast that he does not expect perfection on this first dress; that its purpose is to provide a renewed sense of continuity that may have been lost during the segmented process of middle rehearsals.

The final dress rehearsal should be handled exactly like a full public performance, and the director should not stop the performance except in a case of real emergency. Performers who run into problems should be forced to fight their way through them without any help from the director. Some think that an invited audience can help in this process by giving the performers a response to which they can react. This practice seems to be of questionable value, however, unless very carefully handled. An audience of friends and relatives is likely to be far too responsive and laudatory, and a small, scattered audience will not provide enough response to be meaningful. Some colleges and universities have made it a practice to invite class groups from local high schools to final dress. This often works badly, because the responses of high school students are usually quite different from a general and more mature audience, and this can seriously mislead a cast.

Finally, the director's task during these last two dress rehearsals is to prepare his cast psychologically—to be sure that they are "up" and confident. This is quite dependent upon the director's own attitude. A positive, confident, enthusiastic approach, with commendations given out as they are due, will work wonders on cast morale.

PERFORMANCE

The task of the director does not end with final dress rehearsal. He should continue to meet with the cast before curtain, attempting through his own enthusiasm and confidence to bring them up for the performance, to convince them that they *can* and *will* have a good show. If the cast has elected to do warming up exercises, the director should be present to lead them through this process.

In educational theatre, where the learning experience is the essence of all activity, the director should be present to provide a continuing evaluation, to answer questions, and to act as an impartial (to the degree that he can) observer of the performances. Certainly the most important thing that a director can provide, once a production has opened, is continuing support for the cast. They will need it—and appreciate it.

EXERCISE FOR CHAPTER 9

The following exercise is based on the script for *Headaches, Heartaches, and Innocence Be Damned,* and on the completed Exercises for Chapter 9, numbers 3 through 9:

1. Based on the knowledge you have accumulated about the script, and on the technical information in your groundplan, lightplot, costume designs, etc., create a rehearsal schedule for a Readers Theatre production of *Headaches*. The rehearsal time allotted is four hours per day, five days per week, for a period of six weeks. Break your schedule into early, middle, and late rehearsals, and spell out exactly what will be covered in each rehearsal period. Be especially careful in how you apportion time for technical rehearsals.

RON DIEB

Headaches, Heartaches, And Innocence Be Damned

A ONE-ACT PLAY FOR READERS THEATRE

SETTING:

A space containing several stools, a coat rack, and possibly a small table with cigarettes and an ash tray.

CHARACTERS:

Director, also the Narrator of the play within the play. An extremely fastidious, affected, and humorless man who is far more the frustrated actor and playwright than a director.

Woman, also the Woman in the play within the play. Seemingly cynical and sarcastic, but actually more romantically idealistic than she admits, even to herself.

Man, also the Man in the play within the play. Quite a personable and sincere person who is at all times what he appears to be.

[At rise, the Director/Narrator enters an empty stage and looks out into an empty auditorium. He removes his topcoat, scarf, and gloves, and then takes a script from his briefcase. There is apparent affectation in all of his actions. He begins to pace about as he reads silently from the script, mouthing the lines and gesturing with exaggerated flourish. He pauses from time to time to glance at his watch and to look into the wings as if anticipating the arrival of someone.]

Headaches, Heartaches, and Innocence Be Damned, copyright 1973, by Ron Dieb. Printed by permission of Ron Dieb. This script may not be presented or performed publicly without the written consent of Dr. Dieb, Department of Theatre, California State University, Fullerton, California.

DIRECTOR: *[He verbally begins the following speech several times, giving the speech a somewhat different interpretation each time. During the latter part of the speech, the Woman enters, takes off her coat, and looks impatiently at the Director who is far too caught up in his theatrics to notice her until she speaks.]*

"The time is now—or any time—a yesterday that somehow seemed quite special, an autumn filled with hope, a well-remembered year. It matters little for our purposes here just when what will take place took place because such things as you will see and hear and feel, if you will only give to me your eyes and ears and hearts, should happen to us all at one time or another.

"The setting—suit yourselves—make it an anywhere, a room as familiar as the room in which you sleep, and equally as strange. Oh, there need not be a bed. A chair or two will do. A window to open up the world and to close it out as well. And then the light—yes, that's necessary—a light to illuminate to some extent the figures and the faces of the people in our play, people whom you have never known before and will never know again, because they exist only for us and for themselves during the brief moment in which we share their lives.

"So disregard, for the time at least, yourselves, and think of a girl—a girl both lonely and alone—a girl—"

WOMAN: *[She interrupts the Director who turns and sees her for the first time.]* A girl?

DIRECTOR: Yes, a girl.

WOMAN: I thought I was supposed to play a woman—a sort of freaked-out femme fatale who can't get hold of herself or anyone else.

DIRECTOR: Haven't you read the script?

WOMAN: I tried to. God knows I tried. But I just couldn't get through it.

DIRECTOR: Then obviously it didn't get through to you that the character you're to play only thinks she's a woman when actually she's just an innocent young girl whose head is filled with fiction and whose body pulsates with unsatisfied desire.

WOMAN: Just as I thought. She's oversexed and underexposed.

DIRECTOR: No, no, no. Oh, I do wish you had read the script. I gave it to you a week ago at the audition, and if you were half the actress you said you were, you would have had the professional courtesy to read the script at least once before today's rehearsal.

WOMAN: I told you I tried. But when I got to that part where the woman—or the girl—or whatever the hell she is—starts talking about being all alone in the world, I couldn't go on.

DIRECTOR: And why not?

WOMAN: It just didn't seem reasonable—or real. She's supposed to be beautiful and desirable, intelligent and sensitive. Right?

DIRECTOR: Yes.

WOMAN: Then why should she be alone unless she prefers to be alone? And if she prefers to be alone, why does she feel sorry for herself?

DIRECTOR: She at no time indulges in self-pity.

WOMAN: *[She takes crumbled script out of her purse.]* Oh, no? Well, listen to what she says to the man who lives across the hall, here on page six. "I have no friends, no ailing mother, not even a cat. I'm as alone as anyone could ever be in a world that recognizes only people in pairs." Now come on, who does she think she's kidding?

DIRECTOR: She isn't kidding anyone.

WOMAN: I'll say she's not.

DIRECTOR: She's simply aware of her isolated existence in the world. And she's sharing this awareness with another human being, in an effort to make her isolation more bearable. Don't you understand that?

WOMAN: I'll tell you what I do understand. Your so-called isolated heroine is on the make—

DIRECTOR: No—

WOMAN: —and she's playing on this guy's sympathy so he'll take her in. But he's the one who gets taken. Oh, I know her type all right. It's poor little me this and poor little me that until they get some sucker to the altar and then all hell breaks loose. Little Miss Sunshine becomes a tornado—

DIRECTOR: No, no, no!

WOMAN: Yes, yes, yes! She completely dominates her husband who never quite recovers from the shock that he's married such a woman. But the damage doesn't stop there. Oh, no. In addition to shopping and gardening and playing bridge with the girls, she also finds time to run and possibly ruin the lives of her children, her neighbors, and her friends. God help anyone who is her friend. It's better to be her enemy. At least then you know never to turn your back on her, because she's always fully armed and eager for a target.

DIRECTOR: *[With feigned patience]* Are you quite through?

WOMAN: *[Recovering from her outburst]* Yes.

DIRECTOR: Then I suggest you relinquish the role to someone else—someone who understands the essence of innocence.

WOMAN: Sounds like a cheap perfume.
DIRECTOR: Innocence is never cheap. It is the most precious of virtues, the very jewel of maidenhood which sadly becomes but a memory when once it is fearfully and often tearfully yielded to the male.
WOMAN: You're putting me on.
DIRECTOR: Your cynical attitude doesn't surprise me. Many women—like yourself—consider innocence an unnecessary encumbrance in order to live more easily with its loss.
WOMAN: What most men refer to as innocence is really only strategy. And no one knows that better than your simpering, whimpering little heroine.
DIRECTOR: She is not my heroine.
WOMAN: Did you write the play?
DIRECTOR: The idea for the play was mine, as was the idea for the characters, but a very dear friend of mine wrote most of the script. Oh, I did suggest a scene or two.
WOMAN: I'll bet.
DIRECTOR: But I cannot take the credit for having written it.
WOMAN: Or the blame.
DIRECTOR: Look. It's obvious I made a mistake in casting you. *[Hands her her coat.]* Now do gather your things together and leave before the ladies arrive.
WOMAN: What are you talking about? What ladies?
DIRECTOR: The Daughters of Charlotte Cushman.
WOMAN: Charlotte who?
DIRECTOR: Charlotte Cushman.
WOMAN: *[Still confused.]* Oh.
DIRECTOR: Their president is a second—
WOMAN: Whose president?
DIRECTOR: The President of the Daughters of Charlotte Cushman. She's a second cousin of mine on my mother's side, and she asked if she might bring her ladies to a rehearsal. At the time it seemed an excellent opportunity for them to observe me at work in a rehearsal situation, and I all too hastily agreed.
WOMAN: Just a minute. Let me get this straight. Your cousin's daughters are coming here to watch the rehearsal?
DIRECTOR: They're not my cousin's daughters. My cousin's not even married. She's their president, not their mother.
WOMAN: Then she's not Charlotte What's-Her-Face?
DIRECTOR: Of course not. Her name is Lucretia, and she's my second cousin.

WOMAN: On your mother's side.
DIRECTOR: Precisely. Charlotte Cushman inspired the name of the drama club of which Lucretia is president.
WOMAN: What drama club?
DIRECTOR: *[His patience is at an end]* The Daughters of Charlotte Cushman! Haven't you ever heard of Charlotte Cushman?
WOMAN: She another relative of yours?
DIRECTOR: No, no, no! Charlotte Cushman lived over a hundred years ago. She was this country's first great tragic actress. Her Lady Macbeth was a theatrical milestone. A relative of mine indeed.
WOMAN: All right, all right. What do I know about your family?
DIRECTOR: Or the American theatre. Now do please leave. I don't want them to find you here. That would be embarrassing for us all.
WOMAN: What are you going to tell Cousin Lucretia and all those daughters of Charlotte Who's-It? That you couldn't find a virgin to be in your little play?
DIRECTOR: I'll simply tell them you quite suddenly developed a splitting headache which unfortunately rendered you indisposed.
WOMAN: You must be obsessed with women who quite suddenly develop splitting headaches.
DIRECTOR: What do you mean?
WOMAN: Haven't you read the script either?
DIRECTOR: Of course, I have. I practically wrote every line in it.
WOMAN: Just as I thought. Well, if you'll remember, Miss Lonelyhearts goes across the hall to this man's apartment on the pretense of borrowing an aspirin, of all things, because she says she has a headache.
DIRECTOR: I remember.
WOMAN: Not a deck of cards, a tray of ice, or a martini shaker—not anything reasonable—but an aspirin. Now I ask you, what girl in her right mind would have the nerve to go and ask a perfectly strange man for an aspirin in the middle of the night unless it's not an aspirin at all that she wants but something else?
DIRECTOR: It isn't in the middle of the night. It's early one Sunday morning, and all she wants is an aspirin. I don't see anything the least bit unreasonable about that. She simply wakes up with a headache—
WOMAN: A splitting headache.
DIRECTOR: Yes—and discovers she has no aspirin and therefore goes to borrow one.
WOMAN: Talk about meaningful motivation.

DIRECTOR: Since you lack the proper sensitivity to submerge yourself into the very soul of the heroine, you cannot possibly do the role. I told you that before. Now leave!
WOMAN: Don't get artistic on me. I was just trying to make some sense out of all of this. First, we have this girl with a headache. That's acceptable, I suppose. Which of us doesn't have a headache on Sunday mornings. And she's out of aspirin. It's stupid, but even that I'm willing to buy. But why, if she's as young and innocent as you say she is, why would she go across the hall in just her robe—
DIRECTOR: And pajamas.
WOMAN: Pajamas are negligible. Why would she go across the hall in just her robe—and pajamas—to borrow an aspirin from this unattached male?
DIRECTOR: She didn't know that he was an unattached male. She didn't know that he was a male at all.
WOMAN: But she wanted to find out.
DIRECTOR: All she wanted to find was an aspirin. She merely knocked on the first door she came to.
WOMAN: Why didn't she dress first?
DIRECTOR: Because she's pure at heart—something you wouldn't understand.
WOMAN: I may not be pure at heart, for whatever that's worth, but I've yet to run bare-bottomed up and down the halls of my apartment building.
DIRECTOR: *[Exploding]* She is not bare— *[Tries to calm himself]* Oh, what's the use? This debate is getting us nowhere.
WOMAN: At least it's gotten the girl across the hall.
DIRECTOR: It's a waste of my rather valuable time to stand here trying to convince you of the merits of—
MAN: *[Rushing in]* I'm sorry I'm late, but I had the devil of a time trying to find a place to park. I've never seen so many women—and all of them with hats on.
WOMAN: The daughters are descending like locusts.
MAN: *[Noticing Woman for the first time]* Oh, hello. I don't believe we've met before. But I do remember you from the audition.
WOMAN: *[Reacting favorably to the Man]* I remember you too.
MAN: I thought you read very well.
WOMAN: You did too.
MAN: And I was hoping you'd be cast as the girl.
DIRECTOR: Well, she's just been uncast.
MAN: Why?
DIRECTOR: She doesn't like the play, and she thinks the girl is stupid.

MAN: *[To Woman]* You do?
WOMAN: Not stupid exactly.
DIRECTOR: Stupid was the word you used not five minutes ago.
WOMAN: *[To director]* Maybe I did, but since I'm here I might just as well read through it for the ladies. I wouldn't want them to have put their hats on for nothing.
MAN: What ladies are you talking about?
WOMAN: All those ladies in the parking lot. They belong to our director's second cousin on his mother's side, and they're coming to watch our rehearsal.
DIRECTOR: There isn't going to be a rehearsal. Not today at least. Not until I find someone suitable to play the girl.
MAN: You mean I drove all the way here for nothing?
WOMAN: You can always juggle for them—or, better yet, do a flower arrangement. Ladies' clubs love that sort of thing. Or maybe our esteemed director would read my role. He's so enthusiastic about innocent young maiden headaches. Let him submerge himself into the very soul of this vapid virgin.
MAN: How could he possibly take a woman's role?
WOMAN: He'd probably thrive on it.
DIRECTOR: I've heard all I'm going to take. I do not have to stand here and listen to these insults from someone as insensitive as—
MAN: Stop it! Both of you! Please! *[To Director]* Since we're here, it would be a terrible waste of our time to cancel the rehearsal.
DIRECTOR: I fully appreciate your point of view but—
MAN: How long do we have before the ladies arrive?
DIRECTOR: Fifteen or twenty minutes. They're having coffee and sweet rolls in the lobby now. Lucretia made the sweet roles herself.
MAN: Then we ought to have time to read through at least a few of the key scenes before they come in.
DIRECTOR: *[Indicating Woman]* But she refuses to understand the girl in the play. The rehearsal would be a fiasco. And I not only have my reputation to think of, there's my cousin Lucretia to consider. She's up for reelection next month.
WOMAN: How can anyone understand this girl?
MAN: *[To Woman]* We're actors, aren't we? We're supposed to be able to make real that which is unreal.
WOMAN: This is unreal, all right.
MAN: But that's the challenge of theatre—to become someone you're not. Please try—for my sake. And for Cousin Lucretia.
DIRECTOR: It's no use talking to her. She can't extend her imagination beyond her own jaded little existence.
WOMAN: Whose existence are you calling jaded? Just because I don't

|||||||||||||think like this girl doesn't mean there's anything wrong with the way I do think. At least I know the difference between a believable character and a phony.

MAN: What's so wrong with the girl?

WOMAN: Everything.

MAN: Oh, I don't know. I haven't read the script closely yet, but I thought it was a nice touch the way she went across the hall to borrow an aspirin.

WOMAN: A nice touch? It's dumb. And anyway she doesn't even ask for an aspirin when he opens the door. She asks for help.

DIRECTOR: But she means an aspirin.

WOMAN: Then why doesn't she say aspirin? Here it is on page two. This guy across the hall—fool that he is—asks her in, and she goes in. And incidentally and conveniently he's also dressed just in a robe—

DIRECTOR: And pajamas.

WOMAN: And pajamas. Now not a word has been said about a headache or any other kind of ache. She says, "I hope I'm not disturbing you; but I need your help." To which he replies, "You're not disturbing me at all. Come in." And she goes in. And there they are talking about life and love and loneliness. And that kind of talk between a man and a woman can lead to only one thing.

MAN: It's true they do discover each other.

WOMAN: I've never heard it called that before.

DIRECTOR: But their discovery is spontaneous. It's not the least bit premeditated. Surely you can accept the fact that the man couldn't have known it was this particular girl who was ringing his bell.

WOMAN: Why did he ask her in?

DIRECTOR: Because he's a gentleman, and she did, after all, ask for his help.

WOMAN: Why did she go in? Why didn't she just come out with it there in the hall and say, "Got an extra aspirin?" if that's what she really wanted?

DIRECTOR: *[Thinks for a moment]* The hallway is cold. It's an old apartment building, and hallways always lack adequate heating. Everyone knows that. She goes into his apartment not only to get an aspirin but also to get warm.

WOMAN: This is beginning to sound more like *La Boheme* every minute.

MAN: I think you've got something. Maybe the play should be approached in the spirit of *La Boheme*.

WOMAN: And maybe instead of my going to borrow an aspirin, I should go to borrow an iron lung. That, at least, would have style.
DIRECTOR: The iron lung would be excessive, but the girl does have a death wish.
WOMAN: If I were this girl, I'd have a death wish too.
DIRECTOR: She doesn't actually want to die, but she is lonely and isolated.
MAN: And unloved.
WOMAN: You men. You think that every girl had rather be dead than be without a man.
MAN: I'm not saying that every girl feels that way, but this girl seems to feel just that way. Here on page five she says as much. She says, "Does it really matter when we die—or how we die?"
WOMAN: One minute she wants to get rid of a headache, and the next minute she wants to get rid of herself. How am I supposed to make this kind of person believable?
DIRECTOR: Forget about the headache, and try to concentrate on the girl's loneliness.
MAN: Yes, please. I know you can do it.
WOMAN: *[After a pause]* Oh, all right. I'll try, but it isn't going to be easy.
MAN: That's the spirit.
DIRECTOR: *[To the Woman]* And don't overplay the role. Sincerity, not sensationalism, should be your guide.
WOMAN: *[Very dramatically]* I have never overacted in my life.
DIRECTOR: Well, don't start now.
MAN: Please, you two, no more arguments. We haven't much time as it is.
DIRECTOR: I'm willing to overlook certain personality flaws if our actress is willing to do whatever it is she does.
MAN: Fine. *[The Man begins to direct as well as to act both his role and the Woman's role. Each time he reads one of her speeches, she is stopped from reading it herself.]* Why don't we start with the scene at the top of page five, the scene that leads to the girl's death wish. Let's see—here it is. I begin by asking the girl if she's heard about the woman who lived down the hall. And the girl says, "Yes, I was told last night that she threw herself from the roof of this building." And then I say, "Terrible, terrible. And she was so young." And then you say, "Is she—dead?" And I answer, "Yes. She died on her way to the hospital." Then I ask if you knew her. And you say, "No. I had seen her once or twice at the garbage cans downstairs, but I didn't know her. I wish I had. Perhaps I could have helped

	her. Perhaps she could have helped me." And then after a pause, you continue to say, "It's too late—"
WOMAN:	Who's doing this role? You or me?
DIRECTOR:	And who's directing?
MAN:	I'm sorry.
DIRECTOR:	Apology accepted. *[To the Woman]* Please pick it up with your line about helping the woman who lived down the hall.
WOMAN:	"Perhaps I could have helped her. Perhaps she could have helped me. It's too late now though—for both of us."
MAN:	"Why is it too late for you? You're young and alive. Your whole life is before you."
WOMAN:	"Does my life really matter? Does it really matter when we die? Or how we die?"
MAN:	"It matters to me, but there's little I can do about it. I admit that I find life rather tedious at times, but I have no assurance that death will be any less tedious. Call it vanity, if you will, or the instinct for self-preservation, but I try to exert every effort toward the continuation of my life. I don't smoke or drink, unless I'm unduly provoked. Yoghurt and wheat germ make up the bulk of my diet. And I avoid the freeways whenever possible. What do you do to stay alive?"
WOMAN:	I try my damnedest to avoid scripts like this. My God, I've never heard such dialogue. *[To the Director]* This must be one of the scenes you wrote.
DIRECTOR:	I'm proud to acknowledge what is mine.
WOMAN:	Said the old lady as she kissed the cow.
DIRECTOR:	I beg your pardon.
WOMAN:	Skip it.
DIRECTOR:	Yes, I think I shall. *[To the Man]* Cue her in again please.
MAN:	"What do you do to stay alive?"
WOMAN:	"Nothing particularly. Life isn't that important to me."
MAN:	"Then make it important."
WOMAN:	"Why should I?"
MAN:	"Why? Because we can't give in to the—compelling inertia that characterizes most people."
WOMAN:	"I can."
MAN:	"That's an immoral attitude, if you ask me. But then you didn't ask me, did you?"
WOMAN:	"I'd better go. I've taken enough of your time."
MAN:	"No, please, don't go. Have some breakfast with me. I promise to serve you something other than wheat germ. In fact, I'm not a bad cook."

WOMAN:	"I'm sure you're not, but I never eat breakfast. It makes me sick to my stomach."
MAN:	"Then how about a cup of coffee? I make very good coffee."
WOMAN:	"Coffee makes me nervous."
MAN:	"Milk?"
WOMAN:	"I'm allergic to milk."
MAN:	"What do you drink?"
WOMAN:	"You'll laugh at me, but I drink twenty glasses of water a day."
MAN:	*[Laughing]* How do you stay afloat?
DIRECTOR:	That's not in the script!
MAN:	Sorry.
WOMAN:	"An aunt who raised me always insisted on my drinking that much water every day. I can't seem to break the habit."
MAN:	"What was your aunt? A fish?"
WOMAN:	"No, she wasn't a fish. She was a very wonderful woman."
DIRECTOR:	Cut that line.
WOMAN:	About my aunt being a wonderful woman?
DIRECTOR:	No, the line about your aunt being a fish.
MAN:	It's one of the few funny lines in the script. Why do you want to cut it?
DIRECTOR:	It destroys the scene's delicacy.
WOMAN:	Is that what you call it?
MAN:	Then we might just as well cut the whole bit about the twenty glasses of water.
DIRECTOR:	Yes, cut that too. It's absurd.
WOMAN:	I don't think so. My grandmother was a great believer in water. She never kept count of how many glasses I drank a day, but she always told me that water cleansed the system better than anything.
MAN:	My grandmother believed in prunes—stewed prunes. I hate the thought of them to this day.
DIRECTOR:	Would you two drop your grandmothers and their respective methods of purgation and get back to the play!
WOMAN:	*[To the Director]* Since we're cutting the water line, why don't I just accept a cup of coffee?
DIRECTOR:	Very well. Accept the coffee, and add the line, "Yes, I would like a cup of coffee."
MAN:	"How do you take it?"
WOMAN:	I don't know. *[To the Director]* How do I take it?
DIRECTOR:	You're decidedly a cream and sugar type.
WOMAN:	*[To the Man]* "Cream and sugar, please."

MAN: "One or two lumps?"
WOMAN: *[To the Director]* One or two lumps?
DIRECTOR: Hell, take two, three, twelve! What difference does it make?
WOMAN: I was just trying to submerge myself into the very soul of the heroine.
DIRECTOR: Well, it can't be done with so many lumps of sugar. Now do go on.
MAN: All right. *[He pantomimes the following business]* I pour the coffee—add cream—
WOMAN: Just a dash.
MAN: —and two lumps of sugar.
WOMAN: Make it one. I hate coffee that's too sweet.
MAN: One lump then. And then I say— *[To the Director]* What do I say?
WOMAN: *[Pantomimes taking a sip of coffee]* You can say, "Thank you" after I say how good the coffee is.
MAN: "Thank you." *[To the Director]* Then what?
DIRECTOR: Ask her where she works on page seven.
MAN: Yes, here we are. "Where do you work?"
WOMAN: "I don't."
MAN: "Are you a student?"
WOMAN: "Of what?"
MAN: "Of—anything?"
WOMAN: "No."
MAN: "Where do you come from?"
WOMAN: "Across the hall."
MAN: "No, I mean where were you born? Where's your home?"
WOMAN: "A long way away."
MAN: "Are you—involved?"
WOMAN: "With what?"
MAN: "With some young man—or an ailing mother—or even a cat?"
WOMAN: This next line is against my better judgment, but here goes. "No, I'm quite alone. I have no friends, no ailing mother, not even a cat. I'm as alone as anyone could ever be in a world that recognizes only people in pairs."
MAN: "I didn't mean to pry."
WOMAN: "A person can't very well pry into a vacuum, for that's what I am, you know, a vacuum."
MAN: "Nonsense. You're a lovely young girl. And what's even more important, you're unique."
WOMAN: "There's no particular distinction in being unique. No two things in life are alike. Look at my eyes—"
DIRECTOR: Move closer to him on that line.

WOMAN: *[To the Director]* Innocence be damned, huh?
DIRECTOR: He can't look at your eyes if you're halfway across the room, can he?
WOMAN: *[Moves closer to Man]* "Look at my eyes. You would think they matched one another perfectly, wouldn't you? Well, I can tell you they don't. My left eye is a shade darker than my right, and it's a bit larger too. Would you have noticed that if I hadn't told you?"
MAN: "No, but I—"
WOMAN: "Of course, you wouldn't have noticed. No one ever notices. And I doubt that your eyes match—or your ears, arms, hands, legs, or feet. You just seem to be put together well, but you're not at all. I can see that already. None of us are. We're all the result of cosmological error. We're the living evidence of biological imperfection. And if everyone were aware of this, no one would be as proud of himself as everyone is."
MAN: "My, my, my."
WOMAN: "I'm sorry. I didn't mean to get so carried away."
MAN: "Oh, you needn't apologize. I'm glad you feel that you can express yourself honestly with me. It's a compliment."
WOMAN: "I don't know what came over me. I'm usually terrified of people." *[To the Director]* Even your sweet Aunt Lucretia isn't going to buy that.
DIRECTOR: She's not my aunt. She's my second cousin—
WOMAN: —on your mother's side. I forgot.
DIRECTOR: And what is it you think she isn't going to buy?
WOMAN: That this girl is terrified of this guy—or any guy. Didn't she practically force herself into his apartment? That doesn't sound like she's terrified to me.
DIRECTOR: She's not terrified. That's the point. All of her life she's been afraid of men, but she's finally been able to talk to a man who doesn't frighten her, who doesn't threaten her.
MAN: That makes sense to me.
DIRECTOR: It should to anyone who's thinking. *[To the Woman]* Now if you'll continue with the scene, the character may become clear, even to you. Go back to "I don't know what came over me."
WOMAN: "I don't know what came over me. I'm usually terrified of people."
MAN: "But you're not terrified of me."
WOMAN: "You don't count."
MAN: "Whyever not?"
WOMAN: You're going to be sorry you asked.

MAN: *[Looking at script]* Is that the line?
DIRECTOR: No, of course it isn't. Our actress not only acts—on rare occasions—but she's also ever ready with the all too easy quip, the handy-dandy do-it-yourself witticism when what little talent she has fails to surface.
WOMAN: *[To the Director]* Have I stepped on your cow again? Please forgive me.
MAN: *[Looks at wrist watch]* Look at the time. Can't we get on with it? I'll take it from "—you're not terrified of me."
WOMAN: "You don't count."
MAN: "Whyever not?"
WOMAN: "Because you have the eyes of a little boy, and your fingernails are clean."
MAN: "Don't let my seeming innocence mislead you. I could be out to—"
WOMAN: *[After a pause]* "What?"
MAN: *[Hesitatingly]* "Do you in."
WOMAN: "Why would you want to do that?"
MAN: "I wouldn't. Honestly I wouldn't. But there are those who would—under the circumstances."
WOMAN: "No one's ever wanted to do me in—or out—or under."
MAN: "You sound disappointed that they haven't."
WOMAN: "Not disappointed actually—just resigned."
MAN: "What a peculiar thing to say."
WOMAN: "I'm a peculiar girl—as you said."
MAN: "I didn't say you were peculiar. I said you were unique!"
WOMAN: When what you really mean is that she's nuts!
DIRECTOR: Just read the script as it's written, and do try to avoid any further outbursts of your obtuse evaluations.
WOMAN: It's this girl who's obtuse. She should have a trained psychiatric nurse around the clock. She shouldn't be allowed to just run loose up and down the hall.
DIRECTOR: There is nothing mentally wrong with the girl. She does have an emotional problem, a very common emotional problem known as loneliness.
WOMAN: Does that give her the right to scare this poor, unsuspecting male to death?
MAN: I'm not scared.
WOMAN: Well, you should be with all this talk about no one ever trying to do her in.
DIRECTOR: It's merely her way of indicating her innocence.
WOMAN: It sounds like a proposition to me.
DIRECTOR: Yes, I rather imagine that's what it would sound like to you. But you're not this girl. You haven't her sensitivity, her

Headaches, Heartaches, And Innocence Be Damned 115

	delicacy of thought and action, her childlike ignorance of the ways of the world.
WOMAN:	Thank God.
MAN:	I like this girl. I really do.
WOMAN:	How could you?
MAN:	Because I think she *is* unique, in a kind of kooky sort of way. And I also believe she's innocent. God knows that's an unexpected bonus these days.
WOMAN:	Do you place such a high premium on innocence?
MAN:	I don't know. I used to. Maybe I still do. I haven't really thought about it in a long time.
DIRECTOR:	*[Sarcastic]* Then why don't you think about it after the rehearsal.
MAN:	*[Looking at the Woman]* Yes, I'd guess we'd better get back to the play.
WOMAN:	*[Looking at the Man]* Yes, I guess so.
DIRECTOR:	*[Looks at Man and Woman for a moment]* What's the matter with you two?

[Man and Woman quickly look at the Director]

WOMAN:	Nothing's the matter.
MAN:	Nothing at all.
DIRECTOR:	Then let us proceed with the play. Pick it up with your quivering mouth.
MAN:	*[Puzzled for a moment, then finds the line to which the Director refers]* "Your mouth is quivering."
WOMAN:	"Is it?"
MAN:	"Yes. Is anything—wrong?"
WOMAN:	"No, my mouth always quivers when I'm nervous."
MAN:	"Do I make you nervous?"
WOMAN:	"Oh, no. I make myself nervous. My knees knock, my ears twitch, and my mouth quivers. I can't help it. It's all so unattractive."
MAN:	"Not in the least. I think it's a very attractive mouth."
WOMAN:	"I've never liked it. The shape's all wrong. You'd think I'd be used to it by now."
MAN:	"It's a perfectly shaped mouth."
WOMAN:	"Nothing's perfect."
MAN:	"Then let's say it's better than most mouths I've dealt with."
DIRECTOR:	*[To the Man]* At this point you move quite close to the girl, and you both look into one another's eyes—longingly. *[The Man and Woman comply]* That's it. And then the girl turns

suddenly away from the man and walks to the window on "How long would it take?"

WOMAN: *[Turns from the Man and walks to where the Director indicates the window to be]* "How long would it take?"
MAN: "How long would what take?"
WOMAN: "Would it take a woman longer to hit the street below than a man?"
MAN: "What are you talking about?"
WOMAN: "Could a person squeeze a whole lifetime of living into the time it takes to fall from the top of this building to the street?"
MAN: "I'm sure he'd lose consciousness before he ever hit the street."
WOMAN: "How sad to be denied the last and perhaps the first valid moment of life before life ends forever."
MAN: "What a strange way to look at it."
WOMAN: Strange? Not at all. So few lives have any reality, any excitement, any direction. A plunge from the roof of a building would give a person's life an excitement and a direction known to very few."
MAN: "If you don't care where you're going."
WOMAN: "Don't you see? Each of us craves a moment of monumental power, and how fitting that this moment should come at the end of life rather than somewhere along the way."
MAN: "No, I don't see."
WOMAN: And I don't see either.
DIRECTOR: What is it you don't see?
WOMAN: What this girl is talking about. Does she want the man or does she want to kill herself? She can't have both.
MAN: She's not sure what she wants.
DIRECTOR: Exactly. She's confused—and frightened—both by her impulse to stay with the man and to go to the roof. Each of these choices represents a gamble, an adventure, and she's quite naturally apprehensive. She's afraid of contact—with life and with death because she's had no experience with either.
WOMAN: You mean she's really being honest with this guy?
DIRECTOR: Yes, she is. Believe me. Trust me, and the play.
MAN: If she isn't being honest, we haven't got a play.
WOMAN: Then she really does have a problem.
MAN: But it's a problem that can be solved.
WOMAN: How?
DIRECTOR: Would you like to continue and find out?
WOMAN: Yes. I would.
DIRECTOR: Then take it from "She must be very proud today."

WOMAN:	"She must be very proud today."
MAN:	"Who?"
WOMAN:	"The woman who jumped from the roof. I almost envy her. I envy her determination, her faith in death, and her courage to break the bonds of—how did you say it?—human inertia."
MAN:	"I doubt that anyone could be proud in the city morgue, because that's where she is with the rest of the pathetic, meaningless bodies."
WOMAN:	"But our bodies are meaningless from the moment of their conception. At least death frees us from the confines of flesh and blood."
MAN:	"What's wrong with flesh and blood?"
WOMAN:	"Everything. Our bodies can seldom be depended on to behave as they should. They're subject to countless hazards. They can be bruised, cut, or broken. They have to be warmed in the winter or they catch cold and possibly pneumonia. They have to be cooled in the summer or they perspire and become sticky. They forever have to be washed, and they continually grow weary. Our bodies take over when we don't want them to, and they desert us when we need them most. They have their own desires and motivations which are at best embarrassing and at worst humiliating."
MAN:	"But you can't separate the body from man himself."
WOMAN:	"Why not?"
MAN:	"The mind and body function as one. They're partners."
WOMAN:	"Who are forever in conflict with one another. It's all too exhausting, this constant struggle between our physical process and our mental process. Only in death is the struggle ended and the mind and spirit freed from the inconsiderate and often unnatural desires of the flesh."
MAN:	"There's nothing unnatural about physical desire. It's—well, it's a manifestation of a healthy body. And you should learn to cooperate with your body and its very natural desires."
WOMAN:	"I suppose most men feel as you do about the body and its so-called natural desires."
MAN:	"All men and women who believe in their bodies."
WOMAN:	"But surely there are those among us, like myself, who would gladly eliminate their bodies for the unhampered fulfillment and glorification of mind and spirit."
MAN:	"I doubt it."
WOMAN:	"Then I'm more alone that even I imagined."
DIRECTOR:	Not bad. Not at all bad. I think you're gradually assimilating my concept of the role.
WOMAN:	*[To the Man]* I'm not sure that's a compliment.

MAN: I think he means for it to be.
DIRECTOR: The girl moves slowly toward the window again. *[The Woman continues smiling at the Man and doesn't move, unaware of what the Director has said]* Well, move, can't you? *[The Woman moves to the window]* And with her back to the man— *[To the Woman who continues to face the Man as she smiles at him]* Please turn around! *[She does]* Thank you. —she says—
WOMAN: "There's only one sure way to stop forever this obsession with the phsyical."
MAN: "But I'm not obsessed with the physical."
WOMAN: "Look at Socrates—"
DIRECTOR: Turn to face him on that line.
WOMAN: *[Turns to face the Man]* "Look at Socrates, Cleopatra, Romeo and Juliet. They knew."
MAN: "They knew what?"
WOMAN: "That death was the only answer."
MAN: "Will you stop talking about death. And come away from that window."
DIRECTOR: *[To the Man]* Go to the girl and lead her away from the window. *[The Man does as directed]* Yes, that's nice, very nice. *[To the Woman]* It's your line.
WOMAN: "Answer me one question and then I'll go."
MAN: "But I don't want you to go."
WOMAN: "I must—but first the question. Do you completely accept and desire the physical aspect of the human being?"
MAN: "If it's a simple, honest answer you want, I will say then that yes, to my way of thinking flesh and blood arranged in the proper way is not only satisfactory but at times thoroughly delightful."
DIRECTOR: Good. Now the girl moves to the door as if to leave, and the man stops her and says—
MAN: "Where are you going?"
WOMAN: "What difference does it make?"
MAN: "You're not going—to the roof, are you?"
WOMAN: "Why should I go to the roof?"
MAN: "No reason at all. And yet—"
WOMAN: *[After a pause]* "Yes?"
MAN: "No reason at all. I have—"
DIRECTOR: Pause a moment before "I have an idea."
MAN: "No reason at all. *[Pause]* I have an idea. Why don't you let me take you to lunch? It's a lovely day, and I haven't any plans, and if you haven't—"

WOMAN: "I have no plans. I never do."
MAN: "Good."
WOMAN: "But I think I'd rather be alone."
MAN: "Than with me?"
WOMAN: "Than with anyone" *[To the Director]* Do I mean that?
DIRECTOR: You think you do.
WOMAN: But since I'm getting along so well with this man, why do I want to leave him?
MAN: You don't really want to leave me, do you?
WOMAN: Then I wish I'd say what I mean.
DIRECTOR: You do eventually.
WOMAN: Then by all means, let's get on with it. "I think I'd rather be alone."
MAN: "Than with me?"
WOMAN: "Than with anyone."
MAN: "That's your whole problem. How can you ever learn to appreciate the body for what it is if you refuse to expose your body to—well, to other bodies?"
WOMAN: "Such as yours?"
MAN: "You could begin with mine."
WOMAN: "You're very sweet."
MAN: "That's not a very nice thing to say. I'm certainly not trying to be sweet."
WOMAN: "What are you trying to be? Aggressive?"
MAN: "Sort of."
WOMAN: "Physically aggressive?"
MAN: "You needn't put it quite like that."
WOMAN: "To what extent do you think I should expose myself—or rather my physical self—to your physical self?"
DIRECTOR: *[To the Man]* Closer to her on this next speech. *[The Man moves closer to the Woman]* Closer. *[The Man moves even closer to the Woman]* That's it.
MAN: "You could begin by allowing your body to share some intimate restaurant table with mine—by allowing it to sit beside mine in a taxi—and by permitting mine to help yours across streets and into elevators."
WOMAN: "I'm not crippled—or blind."
MAN: "You admit then that the healthy body is preferable to the unhealthy body?"
WOMAN: "So long as we must have bodies—and it seems we must—I do prefer for my body to function according to my best interests." *[She looks up from her script]* That's the first sensible thing I've said.

DIRECTOR: The man takes the girl's hands. *[The Man takes her hands]* She doesn't pull away. She instead smiles and says—
WOMAN: "Is my mouth quivering?"
MAN: "No. Do I still have the eyes of a little boy?"
WOMAN: "Yes, I'm afraid so."
MAN: "I only think it fair to warn you that the little boy you see in my eyes has been known to disappear when the sun goes down."
WOMAN: "That's all right. Little boys should be in bed after dark anyway."
MAN: "I couldn't agree with you more. Shall we go?"
WOMAN: "Yes. No! I have to dress first. We both have to dress. We're still in our robes—" *[She looks at the Director]* —and pajamas." *[The Director nods with pleasure]*
MAN: *[He steps toward the Woman]* "Is that bad?"
WOMAN: *[She backs away from the Man]* "You must promise to behave."
MAN: "I promise."
WOMAN: "Then you can pick me up in fifteen minutes at my apartment. It's right across the hall."
MAN: "I won't get lost."
WOMAN: "I hope not."
DIRECTOR: The girl hesitates for a moment at the door.
MAN: "Is anything wrong?"
WOMAN: "I feel that I'm leaving something behind."
MAN: "Maybe it's your past."
WOMAN: "Then I'd better hurry before it finds me."
DIRECTOR: She turns again to leave, but the man stops her and says—
MAN: "By the way, what's your name?"
DIRECTOR: The girl looks at him for a moment, smiles, and answers—
WOMAN: "Woman."
MAN: "I knew it. Please hurry."
DIRECTOR: The girl leaves, and the man begins to whistle happily as the play ends.
WOMAN: *[After a pause]* Is that all?
DIRECTOR: Yes.
WOMAN: It's awfully short.
DIRECTOR: It's long enough for now. Oh, I may expand it into a three-act play in the future. Perhaps I'll even add a bit of music here and there to reinforce the mood. But I must be careful. I don't want the play to become excessively sentimental.
WOMAN: Heaven forbid.

Headaches, Heartaches, And Innocence Be Damned   121

DIRECTOR: *[Looks out toward auditorium]* There's Lucretia. *[He waves]* She's bringing in her ladies now. *[To the Woman and Man]* Are we ready? We should begin as soon as they're seated.

WOMAN: *[To the Man]* You know something funny? This girl never did get her aspirin.

MAN: But she did get her man.

WOMAN: I still think she was after him from the beginning. And you tried to tell me she had a headache. She had a heartache.

MAN: And it takes more than an aspirin to cure that.

WOMAN: She's just another scheming woman after all. I knew it all along.

DIRECTOR: Not scheming—lonely.

MAN: *[Smiling at the Woman]* And lovely.

WOMAN: *[To the Man]* Why are you grinning? You're the one who's been deceived.

MAN: I haven't been deceived. I've been wanting to meet just such a girl across such a hall for years. Her headache was my gain—and I hope her gain as well.

WOMAN: But it was a trick. All that talk about death and the mind and the spirit. Why couldn't she have just been straightforward and asked him over for dinner or a drink?

DIRECTOR: Is that what you would have done?

WOMAN: Yes, it is. I resent deception and fraud and—

MAN: Your mouth is quivering.

WOMAN: My mouth never quivers—unless I'm nervous.

MAN: Why are you nervous?

WOMAN: *[Loudly]* I am not nervous!

DIRECTOR: You're shouting, for heaven's sake. Quiet down. The ladies will hear you.

WOMAN: *[Loudly]* I'll shout if I want to! *[Less loudly]* Do either of you have an aspirin? I have a splitting headache all of a sudden.

DIRECTOR: This is a hell of a time for you to get a headache.

WOMAN: I can't help it. I always get a headache when I'm upset.

DIRECTOR: Why should you be upset? They've come to see me.

MAN: *[To the Woman]* It's only a play—and a ridiculous little play at that. You said so yourself.

WOMAN: *[Looking into compact mirror]* But there is an audience out there. How do I look?

MAN: Perfect.

WOMAN: *[Pleased]* No one's perfect.

MAN: Then let's say you're better than most I've dealt with.

WOMAN: Would you please stop teasing me?
MAN: Would you please have dinner with me tonight?
DIRECTOR: Would you please shut up—both of you?
WOMAN: All right. I will have dinner with you. But remember, we're not two characters in a play.
MAN: I'll remember.
WOMAN: We're two adult human beings.
MAN: Man and Woman.
WOMAN: You're teasing again.
MAN: I hope I'm not.
DIRECTOR: Places. We're ready to begin. *[Stage whisper to the Woman and Man]* Get off the stage.
WOMAN: *[To the Man]* I don't even know your name.
MAN: Would "Man" do for now?
WOMAN: Why do you insist on playacting?
MAN: We're on stage, aren't we? And the play is about to begin.
WOMAN: I'll be glad when it's over.
MAN: I hope it never ends. *[He leads Woman off]*
DIRECTOR: *[To audience]* "The time is now—or any time—a yesterday that somehow seemed quite special, an autumn filled with hope, a well-remembered year. It matters little for our purposes here just when what will take place took place because such things as you will see and hear and feel, if you will only give to me your eyes and ears and hearts, should happen to us all at one time or another."

JERRY V. PICKERING

Elijah

[This script is a contemporary Readers Theatre adaptation of the Old Testament materials concerning the Prophet Elijah. It is obviously, in some cases, designed to be humorous, but essentially it is a serious treatment of a heroic man who dared the might of nations in the service of his god. It is the intention of the script to provide Elijah with the humanity that he must have had by avoiding, at least in part, the cliche interpretation of the fire-breathing Prophet from out of the desert.

The setting for the play is quite simple, requiring only three playing levels connected by some sort of stairway—an abstract version of a double-decked pageant wagon and platea. Furnishings and stage decoration should be kept to a minimum. Lighting effects, on the other hand, should be rather complex, with area lighting for each of the three playing areas and a spot for the upper levels. In one case an effect of distant lightning should be used, though it may be replaced by the sound of thunder.

Sound requirements are not difficult. The voice of Deus may be amplified, depending on the reader doing the role. For preshow music, a Gregorian chant may be used. It is obviously of much later origin than the materials of the script, but it is congenial with the semimedieval style of the production. For Jezebel's dance (optional) any appropriate music may be used. A sound effect of distant but powerful thunder may be substituted for the required lightning, or may be used in conjunction with the lightning.

The script may also be produced in a more stationary style, with stools and reading stands. In such cases there should be three reading levels, with Deus and Bonus Angelus on the upper level, Elijah on level two, and the rest of the characters arranged on level three.]

CHARACTERS

Bonus Angelus *Widow*
Deus *Obadiah*
Elijah *Jezebel*
Ahab

NOTE: This script may be presented without payment of a royalty fee.

124   Elijah

[Preshow music should come up full as the houselights dim, and then fade out as a tight spot on the upper level reveals Bonus Angelus]

BONUS
ANGELUS: *[The first part of his speech is delivered as a formal chant]* The Lord is gracious and great; God without beginning and without end. He is maker unmade and all might is in him. The Lord is life and the pathway thereto, and all is as he commands. *Benedicamus Domino.* *[Dropping the formal manner he becomes the backfence gossip]* It was in the thirty-eighth year of Asa, who was then King of Judah, that the evil Ahab, son of Omri, began his reign over Israel. For twenty-two years Ahab reigned out of Samaria, doing more evil in the sight of the Lord than any of the kings before him. Oh, our Lord was most sorely vexed. It was the least of Ahab's crimes that he lived in the sins of Jereboam—and *everybody* knows what *he* did. And then Ahab actually married Jezebel, who was the daughter of Ethbaal, King of the Phoenicians—and *everybody* knows what *she* was like.

And then Ahab turned from the worship of the Eternal Lord God and began to serve and worship Baal. What he did was terrible, and the Lord waxed wroth. Ahab erected a temple to Baal in Samaria, and in the temple he placed Baal's altar. To please Jezebel he also caused to be erected a graven image of Astarte.

Oh, Ahab did more to irritate the Lord God of Israel than all those kings who had preceded him. So, the Lord in his wrath determined to punish Ahab, and to carry God's word to the Israelites he selected Elijah the Tishbite....

[The spot illuminating Bonus Angelus fades and lights come up on the lower level, where Ahab and Jezebel are seated drinking and feasting, and on the second level where Elijah crouches. Jezebel may dance if desired. All freeze except Elijah]

DEUS: *[From the darkness of the upper level]* Elijah! Elijah!

[Elijah looks about in bewilderment. A tight spot comes up on the upper level, revealing God]

Do you know who I am, Elijah?

ELIJAH:	*[Frightened]* No!
DEUS:	I am the Lord God of Israel. *[Pause] Your* God, Elijah.

[Elijah nods in mute though uncertain assent]

	I have selected you as my prophet, and I have a message which you are to deliver to Ahab in the name of the Lord God. Do you understand?
ELIJAH:	Not exactly, God.
DEUS:	You are to tell Ahab that if he persists in his sin—if he does not repent and turn from his evil ways into the path of righteousness—I shall bring a great drought upon the land.
ELIJAH:	Yes, God. I understand. But why do you not appear to Ahab yourself? He would listen to you, but I . . . I don't think he'll listen to me.
DEUS:	Perhaps, in my own good time. I work in mysterious ways. But for now you must deliver my message. . . . Are you afraid, Elijah?
ELIJAH:	Yes, God. Sorely.
DEUS:	Deliver the message, and be not afraid, for you are in the service of the Lord God.

[Light fades upon Deus]

ELIJAH:	*[Croaks]* Ahab! *[A bit louder]* Ahab! *[Summoning up all his courage. Loudly]* Ahab! Hear me!

[Ahab and Jezebel begin to move again]

AHAB: Who is this ragged old man?

[Jezebel shakes her head in bewilderment]

	You should know, old man, that I am Ahab the great, king of kings, ruler of all Israel. My word is law, and to displease me is painful death. Now, knowing this, do you still call upon me?
ELIJAH:	*[Literally shaking with fear]* I have a message that must be delivered, Oh mighty king.
AHAB:	Speak then. Deliver it, but on the pain of death take care that it does not displease me.

[Jezebel may rise and circle teasingly about Ahab while Elijah, shaken, delivers God's message]

Elijah

ELIJAH: *[Haltingly]* As ... as the ... as the Lord God of Israel lives. ... He whom I serve. ... There shall be neither dew nor rain these years, except as I give orders, and a drought will fall upon the land.

[The light fades on the lower level, and Elijah looks wildly about him]

I did as you said, God. Help me!

[Spot on the upper level comes up, revealing God]

DEUS: You did well, Elijah. You are my prophet.

ELIJAH: *[With courage born of fear]* But he'll kill me! Ahab will have me flayed alive, and the dogs will gnaw at my bones.

DEUS: I will save you, Elijah, for you are my prophet, and only I may command your death.

ELIJAH: Thank you, God. *[Shudders]* It is truly comforting to know that it will be you who orders my death instead of Ahab.

DEUS: But you must do as I tell you, absolutely and without question. Is that understood, Elijah?

ELIJAH: Of course it is. I'm no fool. I understand perfectly. Unquestioning obedience.

DEUS: Then do as I tell you and depart from here. Go into the desert and hide yourself at the brook called Kerith, which flows east of the Jordan.

ELIJAH: Into the desert, God? But I don't like the desert. I don't.... It's hot and full of sand and serpents. Must I go into the desert?

DEUS: Without question, Elijah. Without *any* questions. You will drink water from the brook, and I have ordered the ravens to feed you.

ELIJAH: Ugh! I have to eat ravens? I don't think I'll like that either.

DEUS: You are not to eat the ravens. They will bring you food. Farewell, Elijah.

[Lights fade on the upper and second levels. Lights come up on the lower level, which now contains a stunted looking bush and some rocks. Elijah walks out of the darkness of the levels and seats himself on one of the rocks. He is grumbling to himself]

ELIJAH: I don't like the desert. No, I don't like it at all. I *despise* the desert. During the day I burn, and at night I freeze. In the morning the niggardly ravens bring me a crust of bread, in the

Elijah 127

evening a tiny gobbet of goat meat. *[Looks up]* I'm very glad you're with me, God. *[In a lower voice]* But couldn't the ravens come thrice a day, bearing heavy burdens of good, warm food? *[He pauses, then makes a gesture of dismissal]* Aah! Even the brook is drying up. I shall wither and blow away with the endless sand.

DEUS: *[Voice only]* You shall live, Elijah, for you must still do the Lord's work.

ELIJAH: *[Looking about for the source of the voice]* May I leave the desert now, God? I don't like it here at all.

DEUS: You may leave. From here you must go to Zarephath, which belongs to Sidon, and stay there until I summon you. I have ordered a widow there to provide for you.

ELIJAH: *[A happy and somewhat lustful smile]* A widow, God? After three years in the desert I am to dwell with a widow?

DEUS: *[Meaningfully]* A most *good* and *modest* widow, Elijah.

ELIJAH: *[Face falling dejectedly]* As you say, God. I shall go to Zarephath, there to dwell with the *good, modest* widow.

[Lights on the lower level fade and come up on the second level, which has now been set with a minimum amount of simple furniture, appropriate to the house of a poor widow. The widow is in the house, holding a small bundle of sticks]

ELIJAH: Please....

[The widow starts at the sound of his voice]

I expire of thirst. Give me a little water to drink.

[The widow nods]

And as you believe that the Lord God of Israel lives, please give me a bite of food to eat.

WIDOW: I have no food, man from out of the desert, except for a bit of meal in a jar, and a few drops of oil in a flask. *[She indicates the small bundle of sticks under her arm]* I was just gathering wood that I might cook all that is left for myself and my son. I would like us to eat this once before we die.

ELIJAH: *[For the first time beginning to sound like the prophet]* Do not be afraid, woman. Go and do as you have just said; but first make a small cake for me, and then make something for yourself and your son. For this is the promise of the Lord God of Israel, that the jar of meal shall not be used up, nor the flask of oil diminished, before that day when God sends rain, and the drought is off the land.

[The lights fade. The spot comes up on the upper level, revealing Deus]

DEUS: Here you will remain, Elijah, for three years at my command, until it is time to remove the drought and bring rain upon the land.

[Spot fades and the lights come up on the second level, revealing Elijah seated on the level and the widow standing on the stairs]

WIDOW: He is worse than he was yesterday. There is no breath left in him. My son is dying and the Lord has forsaken us. *[She sits and covers her face with her hands]*

ELIJAH: The Eternal God does not forsake those who serve him truly, and who do not turn from him.

WIDOW: Servant of the Lord—you who have come from out of the desert—what have you to do with my life? Have you come here to call God's attention to some hidden, unknown sin of mine? Are you here to have my son killed?

ELIJAH: I will intercede for your son. God will hear me.

[The lights on the upper level come up slowly as he climbs the stairs and kneels beside the small pad where a child rests, hidden by a blanket]

Oh, Eternal my God, have you brought evil onto this widow with whom I am staying by killing her son? *[He bends his head to touch the child and then raises his face to the heavens]* Oh, Eternal Lord God of Israel, let the child's life return to him.

[The child moves under the blanket, and Elijah gently places a hand on him, as if in benediction]

Rest, child, for the Lord is with you. *[To the heavens]* Thank you, God. *[Calling to the widow]* Your son lives. He will soon be well.

WIDOW: Now I know truly that you are a man of God, and that He speaks through your lips. *[Widow freezes]*

DEUS: *[Voice only]* Elijah, it is now the third year of the drought. Go, you, and show yourself to Ahab. When you have done this I will send rain upon the land.

Elijah 129

ELIJAH: Show myself to Ahab? But he'll kill me. He will have me served up in tiny pieces.
DEUS: I am the Eternal Lord God of Israel! Go, Elijah.
ELIJAH: *[Defeated]* Yes, God.

[Lights fade to dark on all levels, and come up on the lower level, revealing Ahab and Obadiah]

AHAB: This drought goes on and on, Obadiah. Famine and pestilence rage in Samaria, and Baal and Astarte do nothing... nothing. Therefore, we must divide up and search the land for a spring or brook. Perhaps we can find grass to keep at least the horses and mules alive, so that the beasts will not be lost to us.
OBADIAH: I will search closely, mighty king, as you command.

[As Ahab exits, Obadiah pretends to search about with exaggerated eagerness. As soon as Ahab is gone, Obadiah drops his pretense of searching]

OBADIAH: Woe is me! Sometimes I think that kings are even greater fools than common men.

[Elijah enters upon the platea and Obadiah, immediately recognizing him, bows low]

Is that you, my Lord?
ELIJAH: I ... I think so. Who do *you* think I am?
OBADIAH: Are you truly the prophet Elijah?
ELIJAH: *[A bit taken aback by this reception]* Yes, it's me. I have come to show myself to Ahab. Go and tell your lord, the king, that Elijah is here.
OBADIAH: Tell me, great prophet, what sin I have committed that you would send me into Ahab's power and make me lose my life under the most painful of circumstances? As surely as the Lord God of Israel lives, there is not a nation or realm where Ahab has not sent in search of you. When you were not found he made the ruler of each nation take formal oath that they had not discovered you—that they were not hiding you. And now you bid me to go and tell him that "Elijah is here?"

Have you not heard that, when Jezebel was slaughtering the prophets of the Eternal Lord God, I hid a hundred of them in a cave, feeding them on bread and water? I saved them.... Well, at least I saved them for a little while. And now you bid

130   Elijah

	me to go to my lord Ahab and tell him that "Elijah is here"! He will put me to death for my pains, and eventually he will destroy you as well.
ELIJAH:	*[Questioningly]* God? Lord God, where are you? Must I show myself to Ahab, only to end a small drought? *[He waits, but there is no answer. To Obadiah]* I'm afraid that there is no choice. I must confront Ahab immediately.
OBADIAH:	On your head be it. *[Exits]*
ELIJAH:	*[Looks reproachfully toward Heaven]* Being your prophet is not an easy job, you know. . . . And it's dangerous, too. It isn't every man who would consent to be a prophet. *[Short pause]* I could have been a farmer. . . .

[Spot comes up on the upper level revealing God]

DEUS:	Your sacrifice is noted, Elijah.
ELIJAH:	*[A bit mollified]* Well, that's something, at least. Now if only Ahab would suddenly drop dead.
DEUS:	He will not die, until struck by an Aramaean arrow, and the dogs will lick up his blood.

[The light fades on the upper level as Elijah shudders. Ahab climbs to the second level]

AHAB:	Elijah! You! You who are the ruin of all Israel!
ELIJAH:	I'm not the one who has ruined Israel. It is you and yours who have forsaken the Lord God to follow and worship Baal. Again I am here to deliver a message to you. . . . *[He bows his head for a moment, as if asking and receiving guidance]*
DEUS:	*[While Elijah is standing with bowed head. Voice only]* Send you now to the ends of the land and gather all Israel at Mount Karmel. Bring your four-hundred and fifty prophets of Baal, and the four-hundred prophets of Astarte who are maintained by Jezebel.
ELIJAH:	*[Raises his head. Beginning to sound like the wild-eyed prophet from out of the desert]* This I command in the name of the Eternal, who is the Lord God of Israel!

[Ahab shrinks from the presence of Elijah. The lights fade on the second level and come up slowly on the upper level as Elijah mounts the stairs. Elijah faces the audience and addresses them as if they represent all of Israel]

People of Israel, how long will you hobble along in this faith and that? If the Eternal Lord is truly God, then follow him. If

Baal is the true God, then worship him. But at least you should know certainly which is which.

I—I alone—am left as prophet of the Eternal Lord God of Israel, while Baal has four-hundred and fifty prophets and Astarte has four-hundred. Their numbers are too great for me to contest with them individually, so I propose a contest. Bring two bullocks and place them out on the plain, laying them on wood but putting no fire beneath them. You call upon your god, and I will call upon the Eternal Lord God of Israel. The god who answers by fire, he is the true god.

[There are cries of assent from those characters who are offstage]

Choose one bullock for yourselves and dress it first—for there are many of you—but put no fire underneath. Then call upon your god to kindle the flames and roast the bullock, and we will have a feast in his honor, for he will have demonstrated that he is the true god and deserving of reverence.

[A call from offstage: "The bullock is ready"]

Call upon Baal, who is your god! If he is truly god, then let him answer.

[From offstage voices call, variously, "Baal," "Great Baal," and "Baal, answer us"]

Shout, for he is a god! Perhaps he is musing, or away on business, or asleep. He must be awakened. Shout! Call to him!

[The offstage voices of the Israelites continue to call upon Baal: "Great Baal, answer your servants"; "Baal, hear our plea"; "Baal, fire the sticks beneath your bullock"]

Close, now! Attend me and hear what I say.

[The Israelites give off their prayers]

While you were praying to Baal, I sent those I can trust to prepare the bullock of the Lord God. It is ready, and his altar, which you allowed to crumble, has been repaired. Water has been poured on the bullock, and on the altar, and water has been placed in a trench about the area of sacrifice. All is in readiness.

[The offstage Israelites, who have been ad libbing to each other sotto voce during this announcement fall silent on the last sentence. Elijah throws open his arms to the heavens]

Oh, Eternal God of Abraham and Isaac! Lord God of Israel! This day be it known that Thou art God in Israel, and that I am Thy servant, and that all this have I done at Thy bidding. Hear me, Lord God, hear me and let these, your people, know that Thou art truly God, and make their minds turn to Thee once more! *[Falls to his knees]* Oh, my God!

[Lightning flashes behind Elijah, and thunder rolls. The offstage Israelites cry out: "The Eternal Lord God lives!"; "He is the true God of Israel!"; "He is the one and only true God!"]

Seize the prophets of the false Baal. Let none of them escape!

[The offstage Israelites cry out: "Seize the false prophets!"; "Let none escape!" Obadiah climbs up to join Elijah on the upper level]

ELIJAH: Go. Look out at the sea.
OBADIAH: *[Looks out toward audience]* There is nothing.
ELIJAH: Look again.
OBADIAH: *[Looks, shading his eyes]* A cloud is rising up out of the sea, small as a man's fist.
ELIJAH: The drought is ended, as God promised. Go and tell Ahab to hasten, lest this rain stop him before he reaches Jezreel.

[Obadiah exits]

End me, God. Strike me down into the dust, for I can stand no more of this. Oh, Lord God, I am mortal, as was my father and his father before him. The concerns of God weigh heavily on me.
DEUS: *[Voice only]* Your time is not yet, Elijah. There is still work for you to do.
ELIJAH: I have been given news of Jezebel.
DEUS: I know.
ELIJAH: She has heard of the deaths of the prophets of Baal and Astarte, and she has announced that as surely as I am Elijah and she Jezebel, she will face death at the hands of the gods if by tomorrow at this time she does not end my life, as I did theirs.

DEUS:	Fear not, Elijah. Jezebel will not harm you. Now, eat and drink, lest the journey prove too much for you.
ELIJAH:	Journey? What journey?
DEUS:	Eat and drink.

[Elijah mimes eating a small cake and drinking from a flask of water]

ELIJAH:	That was very good cake, Lord, and very good water, too—though on the whole water is water and there is very little difference between one sip and another. Still, it was good and I am strong again.
DEUS:	Husband that strength, Elijah. You will need it for your journey.
ELIJAH:	*[Apprehensive]* I will need such strength, God?
DEUS:	You must go to Horeb, which is my mountain, and there take shelter in a cave on the mountainside.
ELIJAH:	Horeb? That is a long journey, Lord.
DEUS:	Indeed it is. It will take you forty days and forty nights, during which time you will neither eat nor drink.
ELIJAH:	*[Protesting]* But . . . but God. . . . *[There is no answer, and so he rises painfully and begins the journey]*

[The light fades on the upper level and comes up on the second level as Elijah walks down the stairs. He speaks mournfully]

    A cave. A bitter cold cave on the side of a mountain. Why couldn't I just once be ordered to wait in a palace? Oh, it's cold, and the wind cuts like a knife.

[Spot comes up on the upper level, revealing God]

DEUS:	What are you doing here, Elijah?
ELIJAH:	*[Confused]* What am I doing here? But. . . . But you. . . . Oh! *[The last is a drawn-out exclamation of real pain]* I have been zealous for you, Eternal God of Hosts. The Israelites have forsaken you, breaking down your altars and killing your prophets. I am the only one left, and they seek me to take my life.
DEUS:	Go outside, Elijah, and stand before me on the mountain.

[Elijah steps forward to the front of the level]

ELIJAH:	I feel a great wind, God, but you are not in it. *[Pause]* I feel

	the earth tremble, but you are not in its trembling. *[Pause]* I see fire, but again you are not there in its heat and light. *[Pause]* I hear a gentle whisper and.... *[Falls on his knees and covers his face]*
DEUS:	What are you doing here, Elijah?
ELIJAH:	I have been zealous for the Eternal God of Hosts. The Israelites have forsaken you, breaking down your altars and killing your prophets. I am the only one left, and they seek me to take my life. Now I am here to do your will.
DEUS:	Go back. Take the desert road to Damascus. When you arrive you shall appoint Hazael to be King of Aram; Jehu, the grandson of Nimshi, to be King of Israel; and Elisha, the son of Shaphat, to succeed you as prophet. Whoever escapes the sword of Hazael shall Jehu slay, and whoever escapes the sword of Jehu shall Elisha slay. I will spare seven thousand men in Israel; all who have never bowed down to Baal. That is my will, Elijah.
ELIJAH:	*[Patient resignation]* Yes, God.

[Lights fade on second level and come up on the lower level, revealing Ahab and Jezebel. Ahab is angry and sullen]

JEZEBEL:	Why are you so depressed, my lord and husband? You didn't even touch your supper, and it was delicious.
AHAB:	I asked Naboth of Jezreel to let me buy his vineyard—I even offered him another vineyard to replace it—and he said he wouldn't sell it to me.
JEZEBEL:	Aren't you even in command of your own kingdom? Get up and eat your supper. I'll get you the vineyard of Naboth.
AHAB:	How? He said that in the name of God he would never give me his property, which was the property of his father.
JEZEBEL:	You asked him to sell to you, and he refused. I shall command... command his death. I will write a letter in your name to the governors of Jezreel. I will tell them to proclaim a fast and a gathering. At the gathering they will have two men confront Naboth and charge him with breaking the fast and cursing God and the king. Then they will take him outside the town and stone him to death. After that you will take possession of Naboth's vineyard, which he refused to let you buy, for he will be dead.
AHAB:	Oh, that is a marvelous plan. Truly you are a queen of queens.

[Lights on the lower level fade. Light comes up on the second level, revealing Elijah]

DEUS: *[Voice only]* Elijah! Elijah, my prophet!
ELIJAH: *[Looks up desperately]* Yes, God.
DEUS: You must leave.
ELIJAH: Again? Must I?
DEUS: You must go to confront Ahab. He is in the vineyard of my servant Naboth, of which he has taken possession. Give him this message from the Lord God of Israel. Say to him, "You have killed, and you have taken possession, have you?" Say to him, "Where dogs licked up the blood of Naboth, there shall dogs lick up your blood."
ELIJAH: *[Weary resignation]* Yes, God.
DEUS: Then go now, Elijah.

[Lights on the second level fade as Elijah walks down the stairs. Lights come up on the lower level, revealing Ahab. Elijah confronts him]

ELIJAH: *[Doggedly repeating the message]* You have killed and taken possession, have you? Where the dogs licked up the blood of Naboth, there shall dogs lick up your blood.
AHAB: So you know what was done to Naboth. . . .
ELIJAH: *[He does not know, and is a bit uncertain]* I . . . I know what was done, and because you have sold yourself to no purpose, doing what is evil in the sight of God, I will bring evil on you. I will cleanse the world of you.

[Ahab freezes]

DEUS: *[Voice only]* You exceed my message, Elijah, but because you are my prophet I will make your words come to pass.
ELIJAH: Thank you, God.

[Ahab begins to move again]

            I will strip Ahab of every male child, and of free and fettered alike in all Israel. Your house will fare like the house of Jereboam, the son of Nebat, and like the house of Baasha, the son of Abijah, for the provocations that have made Israel sin. Anyone belonging to Ahab, who dies in the city, the dogs shall devour him. Anyone who dies out in the country, wild birds will eat him. Finally, the dogs will eat Jezebel in the territory of Jezreel.
AHAB: *[Cries out in real terror]* Bring me sackcloth and ashes, that I may repent of my sins before the Eternal Lord God of Israel! *[Freezes]*

136   Elijah

[Spot on upper level comes up, revealing God]

DEUS: Elijah, do you see how Ahab humbles himself before me?
ELIJAH: Yes, God.
DEUS: As he humbles himself before me, I will not bring evil in his reign. I will bring evil on his house during his son's reign. *[Pause]* It is over, Elijah, my prophet. Ahab is humbled and Shaphat will now succeed you to carry my word to the people of Israel.
ELIJAH: Did I do well?
DEUS: You did well, Elijah, in my sight.
ELIJAH: *[Kneels]* Thank you, God.

[Music comes up lightly. Lights fade slowly to black]

TRANSLATED AND ADAPTED
FOR READERS THEATRE
BY JERRY V. PICKERING

The Farce of Master Pierre Pathelin

[This play is deservedly the most famous of all the medieval farces, and certainly one of the best farces written during any period. It is especially impressive and unusual in that the largest part of its humor comes from the lines and characterizations and not from the slapstick and pratfall so common to this genre. As a wry comment on lawyers, judges, and the law, it has never been equalled; as a perceptive statement on the essential cupidity of human nature it is in a class by itself.

The script may be performed in concert theatre style or in the more stationary classic style, with stools and reading stands. In the latter case the indicated entrances, exits, and scene changes may be handled by changes in lighting or by any of several methods discussed in this book. Physical actions called for in the script, even Pathelin getting in and out of bed, can be transmitted to the audience through suggestive movement.

It should also be noted that in one production the character of the Draper was changed from male to female (with only minor script revisions) with great success. Also, the role of the Shepherd was read by a girl.]

CHARACTERS

Pierre Pathelin,	a shyster lawyer
Guillemette,	a nagging wife *with cause*
Draper,	a tightwad cloth merchant
Shepherd,	employee of the Draper, sheepstealer, and client of Pathelin
Judge,	a legal simpleton

NOTE: This script may be presented without payment of a royalty fee.

I

The House of Pathelin

PATHELIN: Holy Mary, Guillemette, you know how hard I try to make a little money from my work, and yet I can't put two francs together at one time. I used to have plenty of clients. Plenty of them.

GUILLEMETTE: By Our Lady! The way you carry on about your nonexistent clients. You know what your trouble is? Nobody ever thinks about you anymore. I can remember when everybody wanted to have you argue their cases in court, but now you're known as the Aimless Advocate.

PATHELIN: Just the same, and I don't say it to boast, there isn't a cleverer man than me in the whole district—except maybe the Mayor.

GUILLEMETTE: That's because he's been reading up on his grammar. He wants to become known as a scholar someday.

PATHELIN: There isn't a case I couldn't win if I put my mind to it, and I'm not even an educated man. I swear, I can sing a part in the choir in perfect Latin, right along with the priest.

GUILLEMETTE: Singing Latin in the choir won't put food in our bellies! We're starving to death! Our clothes are all worn out . . . I don't know where we'll get new ones. And you brag about your learning!

PATHELIN: Hold your tongue, woman! Is that all? New clothes? All that takes is a little thought. We'll make out, God willing. There's nothing that changes faster than luck, and there's no one who's my equal when it comes to something like this.

GUILLEMETTE: By the holy saints, not at swindling. At that, you're the master.

PATHELIN: Only at honest arguing, as God is my witness. I'm nothing but an honest lawyer.

GUILLEMETTE: No, by my faith, you're not an honest lawyer but a master of deception. You want to know the truth? I have to admit it. You're no scholar—you haven't even got common sense—but everybody agrees that you've got the sharpest wits in all the parish.

PATHELIN: That's true. There aren't many people who have such a keen knowledge of the finer points of the law as I have.

GUILLEMETTE: Or the finer points of cheating, by God! You're well known for that, all right.

PATHELIN:	What I've done is no worse than those lawyers who dress themselves up in fine clothes and claim to be experts on the law when they don't know a thing about it. Ahhh! This nonsense gets us nowhere. I'm going to the marketplace.
GUILLEMETTE:	The marketplace?
PATHELIN:	Yes, by Saint John, to the marketplace. *[He hums]* Hi, ho, I'm off to the fair.... *[To Guillemette]* Will it displease you if I buy enough cloth for use in our household? Our clothes are falling apart.
GUILLEMETTE:	Buy? But you haven't got a cent.... Have you?
PATHELIN:	Haven't I, sweet lady? If I don't come back with a piece of cloth big enough for the two of us, you can call me whatever names you want. What color would you like? Dark green? A bit of lace from Brussels? What do you fancy?
GUILLEMETTE:	Whatever you can get. After all, beggars can't be choosers.
PATHELIN:	*[Counting on his fingers]* For you, two yards and a half. For me, three. Perhaps four. That makes....
GUILLEMETTE:	*[Interrupting]* You count off yards very generously, but where the devil will you get it?
PATHELIN:	Why do you ask that? Just leave it to me. I'll get it, I promise you that, and I'll pay for it ... on judgment day.
GUILLEMETTE:	Ah ha! On that point I agree. You'll cheat someone.
PATHELIN:	I'll buy grey or green. For underwear I'll need three quarters of a yard of brown ... or maybe a yard....
GUILLEMETTE:	*[To Heaven]* He really thinks he's God! Don't go to the tavern unless you can find someone to pay for your drinks.
PATHELIN:	Take care. *[He exits]*
GUILLEMETTE:	*[Calling after him]* What merchant do you think will...? Pray to the good God that you don't get caught!

II

In Front of the Draper's Stall

PATHELIN:	I wonder if he's in. I'll make sure. Why, by the Sainted Mary, there he is, skulking about in there among his bolts of cloth. *[Calls to the Draper]* God be with you!
DRAPER:	God give you joy.
PATHELIN:	And that he has, for I've been wanting to see you quite badly. How's your health?
DRAPER:	Good, by God!

PATHELIN:	Your hand, then. How goes it?
DRAPER:	Better than I can say. And you?
PATHELIN:	Never better, by Saint Peter the Apostle. How's business?
DRAPER:	Well enough. But we merchants, as you well know, don't always get everything our way.
PATHELIN:	How do you manage to sell merchandise if you don't take care of yourself and eat?
DRAPER:	Ha! Before God, my good friend, it isn't always easy to make ends meet.
PATHELIN:	Now a really clever man, God rest his soul, was your father. Sweet Mother Mary! He was just like you, you know. A good and careful merchant, he was. And you're a lot like him; his very image, I swear. May God rest his eternal soul.
DRAPER:	Amen! And ours too, by His grace.
PATHELIN:	I swear that many a time he warned me, at great length, of what things were coming to. Many a time. It's true . . . everybody loved him.
DRAPER:	Sit down, sir. It's a good time to tell you, most graciously, that . . .
PATHELIN:	I'm comfortable as I am, by God's precious body! It's true, he had . . .
DRAPER:	Truly, you must sit.
PATHELIN:	Well, thank you. . . . Ah! Now I can tell you some of the grand and marvelous things he told me. *[Peers closely at Draper]* Before God! Your ears, nose, mouth, eyes! Never was a child so like his father. You even have his cloven chin. You're him to the life. You're your father's child, if ever a man was! I can't understand how nature could create two faces so much alike, right down to the last detail. You're as much alike as two peas in a pod. You even have the same manner. . . . And your dear Aunt, Laurencia, has she passed away?
DRAPER:	No. Not as far as I know.
PATHELIN:	Ah, the things I could relate about her beauty, honesty, and graciousness. By God's precious Mother, you look like her, too! Such a family for looking like one another. The more I look at you . . . *[Stares fixedly at the Draper]* By God, you're the very image of your father! You're as alike as two drops of water, no doubt about it. And what a good fellow he was, that wise old bird! We had a lot of laughs together, the two of us. If there were more people like him there'd be less robbery and treachery in the

	world, you can take my word for that. *[He picks up and feels a piece of cloth]* What a fine piece of cloth this is. So soft and supple....
DRAPER:	I had it specially woven, from the wool of my sheep.
PATHELIN:	Ah ha! What a manager you are! You're your father all over again.... Always busy. With you it's always business.
DRAPER:	What else can a man do? If you want to earn a living you've got to get your back into things.
PATHELIN:	*[Touching another piece]* This cloth! Is it dyed? It's strong as leather.
DRAPER:	It's a very nice bit of cloth from Rouen, and I assure you it's very well woven.
PATHELIN:	I must say, I've taken a liking to it. By the passion of our Lord, I hadn't intended to buy any cloth when I came in, but I've put aside eighty gold crowns to invest in some property and I can see that I'm going to spend twenty or thirty of them with you. I just can't resist the color, you know.
DRAPER:	Gold crowns? Indeed! If you buy some cloth, maybe the people you're investing with would take their payment in silver.
PATHELIN:	They very well might. I could find out. Gold or silver, it's all the same to them. *[He touches a third piece]* What a piece of cloth! The more I see it, the more I want it. I really must have a tunic made of it, and my wife must have one, too.
DRAPER:	Certainly you can have some of it if you want. But I'm afraid you won't be too happy with the price. Ten or twenty francs won't buy very much.
PATHELIN:	Even if it's expensive, it's worth the price. I still have a little nest egg that nobody knows about.... Not even my wife.
DRAPER:	God be praised! By the sainted Father, I'm glad to hear it!
PATHELIN:	In a few words, I like this cloth so much that I must have some of it.
DRAPER:	All right. Tell me how much you want. Don't be afraid to take as much as you need. The whole bolt is yours, and you don't have to worry about cost.
PATHELIN:	That's very good, thank you.
DRAPER:	Do you like this light blue?
PATHELIN:	Before I decide, how much is it per yard? But wait a moment ... God shall have the first payment. That's only

	right. Here's a sou for the alms box. We must do everything right and proper, in God's name.
DRAPER:	By God, you're a good man. Thank you. Now, about the price.... Shall I tell you my last word?
PATHELIN:	Yes.
DRAPER:	It will cost you just twenty-four sous per yard.
PATHELIN:	Twenty-four sous? Holy Mother!
DRAPER:	That's what it cost me. By my soul! I'll have to replace what you buy.
PATHELIN:	No. It's way too much.
DRAPER:	But you don't realize how much the cost of cloth has gone up. So many sheep have been killed this winter by the heavy frosts.
PATHELIN:	Twenty sous! Twenty sous!
DRAPER:	I tell you, I can't take a penny less. Just wait till market day and then you'll see the price of cloth. By my oath, fleeces which used to be plentiful and cost only twenty francs now cost me eighty.
PATHELIN:	Well, if that's truly the way it is then, without more debate I'll buy. Come on, measure it.
DRAPER:	How much do you want?
PATHELIN:	That's easy to figure out. Let me see.... Three yards for me, and for my wife—she's tall—two and a half yards. That makes, well, six yards. But no, that's only ... What a fool I am!
DRAPER:	You'll only need an extra half yard to make it an even six.
PATHELIN:	I'll take the whole six yards, then. Anyway, I need a hat.
DRAPER:	Take hold and we'll measure it. They need holding down. *[They both measure]* There's one ... and two ... and three ... and four ... and five ... and six.
PATHELIN:	By Saint Peter's belly! Accurate to the last yard!
DRAPER:	You didn't think I'd short you?
PATHELIN:	Oh, no. There's always the chance of a little gain or loss when you buy something. How much is it altogether?
DRAPER:	We'll figure it carefully. At twenty-four sous for each yard, and at six yards, that's nine francs.
PATHELIN:	That's for the whole thing? Nine francs ... that's six crowns, you said?
DRAPER:	Truly. Before God!
PATHELIN:	Then, sir, I must ask you to give me credit until you come by my place. *[The Draper frowns and Pathelin, seeing it, hurries on]* But it isn't really a matter of credit, after all.

The Farce of Master Pierre Pathelin 143

	I'll pay you in gold or silver just as soon as you come to my house.
DRAPER:	By our sainted Mother! That's considerably out of my way.
PATHELIN:	Why didn't you mention that before? You're absolutely right! It is out of your way. Ah! I know what. You've never had a reason to come and drink with me before. Well, here's your chance!
DRAPER:	By Saint James, I never seem to do anything else than drink. Oh, well, I'll come along, but I don't like giving credit, you know, as short of cash as I am.
PATHELIN:	Why, aren't you satisfied with being pressed to accept gold coins instead of silver? By God, we'll even have the goose that my wife was roasting when I left.
DRAPER:	*[Aside]* He's a real pest, this fellow! *[To Pathelin]* Not so fast. I'll bring the cloth along as soon as I can.
PATHELIN:	Absolutely not! I wouldn't want to burden you. I'll just tuck it under my arm.
DRAPER:	But you shouldn't have to.... It's only fair that I should carry it.
PATHELIN:	Saint Mary damn me if I put you to the trouble! *[He puts the cloth under his arm]* There it is, under my arm. It's a real prize.... This will be wonderful. We'll have plenty to drink—and plenty to laugh about—before you go home.
DRAPER:	And you'll give me my money just as soon as I arrive?
PATHELIN:	Pay you? Of course I'll pay you, by God! But not until you've had your delicious meal. In fact, I'm glad that I wasn't able to pay you at this time. Now you'll be able to come and sample my wine cellar. Your old father, now, he never passed my house without a "My friend!" or a "How are you?" or a "What are you doing?" But the rest of you rich people, you don't give a damn about the poor.
DRAPER:	By the saints' blood, I'm one of the poor ones!
PATHELIN:	All right. Goodbye! Goodbye! Come along just as soon as you can. We'll have a fine drink, I promise you.
DRAPER:	All right, then. You go on ahead and get my money ready.

[Pathelin moves away toward his house]

| PATHELIN: | *[Aside]* Money! How about that? Money! The devil take him and his money! I'll see him hanged before I pay him! He sold at his price and he'll be paid at mine. He's short of |

money? God's tears! If he had to run from now till he gets paid, he'd find himself in Barcelona first! *[He exits]*

DRAPER: *[Alone]* They'll be hidden away, these crowns of his, that's for sure. He probably stole them from me. He may be good at buying, but I'm better at selling. The fool was silly enough to pay twenty-four sous per yard for cloth that's not even worth twenty! *[Exits]*

III

The House of Pathelin

PATHELIN: Well? Where is it?
GUILLEMETTE: What?
PATHELIN: Your old, worn out dress.
GUILLEMETTE: Why do you have to ask? I'm wearing it! *[Suspiciously]* What have you done?
PATHELIN: Nothing! Nothing! I just thought I'd make you a little curious. *[He uncovers the cloth]* Didn't I tell you? How's that for a piece of cloth? There!
GUILLEMETTE: Sacred Mother! On the hazard of my life, he goes around with that under his arm. Did you steal it? *[Wailing]* Ohhh! Who'll pay for it?
PATHELIN: How can you even ask? It's already paid for, by Saint John! The Draper that I bought it from wasn't as foolish as all that, sweetheart. May I be hanged if I haven't bled him white as a sack of plaster. The miserable rag-picker! Oh, I've carved him up nicely!
GUILLEMETTE: What did it cost you?
PATHELIN: It cost me nothing. He's paid, so forget about it.
GUILLEMETTE: But you didn't have any money! He's been paid? With what money?
PATHELIN: Ha! Even if I'd had a franc, woman, I wouldn't have given it to him.
GUILLEMETTE: Good luck! Did you sign a promisory note? Is that how you got it? And when the money comes due the bailiffs'll come down on us and take away everything we've got!
PATHELIN: By the sacred blood! I paid only a sou for the whole thing, and that's the truth of it.
GUILLEMETTE: *[Sarcastically crossing herself]* Benedicite Maria! Just one sou! *[Sternly]* That can't be the truth!
PATHELIN: May I be struck blind if I paid more than that, and the Draper can whistle for his money.
GUILLEMETTE: Who was it?

PATHELIN: It was Guillaume, if you must know.
GUILLEMETTE: But how did you get it for one sou? What was the game?
PATHELIN: The sou was God's sou, for the public alms box, and when I asked him to drink on it he asked first for his money. It was a labor of love. He and God can share the sou between them if they like, for it's all the money he'll get. He can raise the roof, or do whatever he likes. It'll do him no good.
GUILLEMETTE: How did you get him to trust you?
PATHELIN: By our beautiful mother, I praised him so much that he nearly gave it to me. I told him what a fine fellow his father was. "Ah," said I, "you come from a fine family. Your family," said I, "is easily the best in the whole neighborhood." But I swear to God that he has all the charm of a poltroon. I swear that he's the ugliest rascal in the whole country. "Ah," said I, "my good friend Guillaume, how much you resemble your father, in your face and in every other way!" God knows, I piled on the flattery and then I threw in something about his cloth. "And also," said I, "your father was so generous in giving credit to his customers." And then I added, "Of course, he was the spitting image of you." But you knew his father as well as I did. You could pull the very teeth out of the miserly old rascal, just as you could out of his son, before they'd lend one sou to a poor soul or even say Hello to their dearest friend. . . . I turned him bottom-side up, tying him up with words, and in the end he gave me six yards on credit.
GUILLEMETTE: And when must you pay?
PATHELIN: Pay? I'll pay him the devil!
GUILLEMETTE: It reminds me of the story of the crow, who was seated high on a branch with a cheese in its beak. Along came a fox who saw the cheese and said to himself, "How can I get it?" Then, from below the crow, he said, "Ha! Some birds have the most beautiful feathers, and their song is sweet and melodious." The crow, proud of his heritage, began boastfully to sing, but when he opened his beak to sing the cheese fell to the ground, where the fox jumped on it and carried it away. And you were the fox, eh? Full of flattery and fine words? And he just let the cloth fall into your hands!
PATHELIN: He's coming here to eat some of the goose you cooked. I'm sure he'll demand his money as soon as he arrives, for which case I have an excellent plan. I'm going to get into

	bed as if I were ill. When he comes, you must say, "Ssh, speak softly," and then sigh and look pale. "Alas," you say, "he's been ill for two months." And if he says, "He's a deceiver, he's only just left me," you must reply, "This is not the moment for your jokes." Then you can leave it all to me. I'll sing him a pretty tune.
GUILLEMETTE:	By my faith, I'll play my part, but if anything goes wrong and he takes us to court, I'm afraid it'll go a lot worse for us than it did last time.
PATHELIN:	Be quiet! I know what I'm doing. You just do as I say.
GUILLEMETTE:	Before God, have you forgotten the Saturday when they put you in the pillory? You know what everybody said about you and your trickery.
PATHELIN:	True, they cast aspersions.... But he'll be here soon, and we've got to keep this cloth. I'm going to bed.
GUILLEMETTE:	Go, then!
PATHELIN:	Don't you dare laugh!
GUILLEMETTE:	Laugh? I'll cry hot tears.
PATHELIN:	You mustn't weaken or he'll suspect.

IV

Before and Then In the House of Pathelin

DRAPER:	Hello, Master Pierre!
GUILLEMETTE:	*[Appears at the door]* Sir, for God's sake, if you have something to say, speak more softly.
DRAPER:	God protect you, madam.
GUILLEMETTE:	More softly!
DRAPER:	Why?
GUILLEMETTE:	Common courtesy, sir.
DRAPER:	Where is he?
GUILLEMETTE:	Where should he be?
DRAPER:	Where?...
GUILLEMETTE:	Ha! That's the sad part of it. Where is he, indeed? God in his grace, understands, and He guards the place where my husband is, the poor martyr.... Eleven weeks without moving!
DRAPER:	Who?
GUILLEMETTE:	Why, Master Pierre!
DRAPER:	Ahhh! Didn't he just bring back six yards of cloth?
GUILLEMETTE:	Who, him?
DRAPER:	He just left me, not more than a quarter of an hour ago.

	God save me! I'm arguing too much. Just give me my money and no more fooling around.
GUILLEMETTE:	Ha! No more fooling indeed! This is hardly a time to fool around.
DRAPER:	Are you mad? My money! He owes me nine francs.
GUILLEMETTE:	Guillaume, we're hiding nothing here. Why are you bringing your taunts to me? Go blather to some fool who's in a better mood.
DRAPER:	May God strike me down if he doesn't owe me nine francs!
GUILLEMETTE:	Alas, sir, everyone isn't as ready to laugh and joke as you are.
DRAPER:	I pray you, speak sensibly. I've had enough nonsense, madam. Please bring Master Pierre to me.
GUILLEMETTE:	Don't you understand? Even yet?
DRAPER:	But isn't this the house of Master Pierre Pathelin?
GUILLEMETTE:	Yes indeed. The evil Saint Mathelin must have destroyed your mind. Speak softly.
DRAPER:	The devil take you! Will you do as I ask?
GUILLEMETTE:	May God protect me! Softly, softly, unless you want to wake the poor man.
DRAPER:	What? Softly? Do you want me to whisper in your ear, or make signs, or go down to the cellar and talk?
GUILLEMETTE:	By God, you're a great babbler all right, and you always were.
DRAPER:	The devil I am! I'm out of my mind! What do you say? What is the truth? I don't get the point of all this. Truly, Master Pierre took six yards of cloth from me today.
GUILLEMETTE:	*[Raising her voice]* Is that so? Is that a fact? The devil take you! How "took"? I wish they'd hang people who lie! He's in such a state, the poor man, that he hasn't been out of his bed for the last fourteen weeks. Are you making fun of me? What's your reason? Leave my house. For the love of God, leave me alone!
DRAPER:	You tell me to speak softly.... Sacred Mother, you're screaming!
GUILLEMETTE:	*[Softly]* It is you, by my faith, who is speaking so loudly.
DRAPER:	I say, if you want me to go, then give me my money.
GUILLEMETTE:	*[Screaming]* Speak softly! Understand?
DRAPER:	But you're the one who'll wake him up; you're speaking four times louder than I am, by heaven. I insist that you pay me.
GUILLEMETTE:	God in heaven! Are you drunk or are you mad?

DRAPER: Drunk? Plague of the Pope, but that's a nice idea!
GUILLEMETTE: Alas, more softly! Speak lower.
DRAPER: Madam, I demand my money for six yards of cloth, or by Good Saint George . . .
GUILLEMETTE: *[Softly, then screaming]* You're dreaming. Who did you give it to?
DRAPER: To him.
GUILLEMETTE: He's in good shape to need cloth! Alas, the only cloth he'll need is the white one he's going to be wrapped in; and he won't leave the house again until he goes out through the door feet first.
DRAPER: But as surely as the sun rises in east, I just spoke to him today. Truly. . . .
GUILLEMETTE: *[In a piercing voice]* You have a very high voice! Please speak lower!
DRAPER: It is you, by my faith! You're screaming as if you're on the bloody stage. Just pay me and I'll go. By God, every time I've given credit it's gone this way!
PATHELIN: *[From his bead; beginning to rave]* Guillemette! A little rose water! Lift me up so that I can sit. Pretender! Who am I talking to? It's the water jug! Rub the soles of my feet!
DRAPER: I can hear him now.
GUILLEMETTE: Truly.
PATHELIN: Ha, you evil woman, come here! Haven't I told you to open these windows? Come and cover me up! Who are these shadow people? Marmarra, carimari, carimari! Take them away from me! Take them away!
GUILLEMETTE: *[Enters the house]* What's this? How you carry on! Have you lost your senses?
PATHELIN: Can't you see what I perceive? *[He is agitated]* There's a black monk flying around the room. Catch him! Bring a crucifix! Get the cat! See how he rises!
GUILLEMETTE: What's all this? *[Calls to the Draper]* Aren't you ashamed of yourself? By God, you've got him much too excited.
PATHELIN: *[Relapsing into exhaustion]* The doctors are killing me with their foul mixtures that they give me to drink. But you have to take their word. You're like putty in their hands.
GUILLEMETTE: *[To the draper]* Alas! Come and see, good sir! He's suffering very badly!
DRAPER: His sickness comes at a good time! Did he fall ill the moment he returned from the market?
GUILLEMETTE: From the market?

The Farce of Master Pierre Pathelin   149

DRAPER: Yes, by Saint John, I met him there. *[To Pathelin]* I want my money for the cloth that I advanced to you, Master Pierre.

PATHELIN: *[Pretending to take the Draper for a doctor]* Ah, Doctor Jean, I've passed two small turds, harder than rocks and round as balls. Shall I take another purge?

DRAPER: What do I care? I can't do anything about it. It's nine francs that I want.

PATHELIN: I have little black things here. Do you call them pills? Should I chew them before swallowing? Before God, don't make me take any more of them, Doctor Jean. They make me throw up. Ohhh, there's nothing more bitter.

DRAPER: No more, for the love of God! You haven't paid me my nine francs.

GUILLEMETTE: It's my opinion they ought to hang people who are so obstinate! Go consort with devils and leave this place of God!

DRAPER: By the God who made me, I want my cloth before I go . . . or my nine francs.

PATHELIN: And me? You don't say anything about what's going to happen to me. Before God, I'd rather anything than pass away!

GUILLEMETTE: Go away! It's an evil thing to pester him to death.

DRAPER: Mother of God, but this is a mess! Six yards of cloth! Now I ask, by your faith, do you think I lost them?

PATHELIN: If you could only give me a purge, Doctor Jean. It's so painful that I can't endure many more hours.

DRAPER: I want my nine francs quickly, or else, by the great Saint Peter of Rome . . .

GUILLEMETTE: Alas, stop tormenting the man! How can you be so cruel? You can see clearly that he thinks you're the doctor. Oh, he's a poor Christian who has had evil fortune. Fourteen weeks without a break he's been lying in that bed, poor man!

DRAPER: By the saints' toenails, I don't see how this can have happened to him. We met this morning and did business together. *[Doubtfully]* At least, I thought that's what happened. Maybe . . .

GUILLEMETTE: By Our Lady, my good sir, you have a bad memory; truly, I advise you to go and rest a little. Besides, you know how the gossips will say that you came inside here on my account. Please go. Any minute now the doctors will arrive.

DRAPER: I don't care what evil the gossips think, for I think nothing! *[Aside]* And, plague take it, I'm getting nowhere. *[To Guillemette]* By the good God, I smell goose....

GUILLEMETTE: What?

DRAPER: Don't you have a goose on the fire?

GUILLEMETTE: That's a nice thing to say! Ha, sir, that's no food for invalids. Go and eat your own goose without playing this stupid game with me. By my faith, you're too nasty for anything.

DRAPER: I beg you not to take it badly; I really thought I smelled goose cooking....

GUILLEMETTE: Still?

DRAPER: By heavens! Before God! I know perfectly well that I should have six yards all in a piece ... if he hasn't got it. But this woman, she mixes me all up. I'm sure he had the cloth. But, by the beautiful Saint Mary, he can't have had it. The whole thing doesn't make sense. Still, I've seen him on the brink of death, unless he was just acting.... That's it! He has got the cloth! He took it this morning and went off with it under his arm! And yet, am I dreaming? Did I give him the cloth? Asleep or awake, I wouldn't give credit to anyone, not even to my best friend. He's got it! No, by God, I know he hasn't! Hang me for a fool if I know who's got the best or the worst of it, him or me. I can't make it out at all! *[Exits]*

PATHELIN: Is he gone?

GUILLEMETTE: Quiet, I'm listening! He was talking to himself as he left, but I can't hear him any more. He was really grumbling, as if he were talking in his sleep.

PATHELIN: Is it all right for me to get up? Has he gone away?

GUILLEMETTE: I'm not sure that he won't come back. No, no, don't even stir. *[Pathelin lays back down]* Our case is done if he finds you out of bed.

PATHELIN: That fixes him nicely, the old rascal. He deserves to be crucified.

GUILLEMETTE: And he's such a greedy old rascal, too. It's poetic justice. You know, he never gives a sou to the collection on Sundays! *[She laughs]*

PATHELIN: For God's sake, stop laughing! If he comes back we're done for, and I wouldn't be surprised if he did.

GUILLEMETTE: *[Trying to choke back her laughter]* By my faith, I'd stop if I could but I can't do it!

The Farce of Master Pierre Pathelin 151

DRAPER: *[Before his stall]* By the sun that shines in the sky, I shall return to the house of this shyster lawyer, and, by God, he'll pay me what's due for what I sold to him. An investor is he? With a nest egg that no one knows anything about? By Saint Peter, he took my cloth by cheating! I gave it to him right here.

GUILLEMETTE: *[Still giggling]* When I think of the face he made when he saw you, it makes me laugh! He was so ardent in his demands. . . .

PATHELIN: Stop laughing! Just smile. He'll be back for sure, and if anyone overheard you we'd be in real trouble.

DRAPER: *[In the street]* He's the lawyer of drinking, the advocate of theft! Does he take all people for Guillaumes? He deserves to be hung, the heretic! He has my cloth, I know it! *[Working himself into a temper]* I've been beaten! *[He returns to Pathelin's house]* Hello! Where are you?

GUILLEMETTE: *[Softly]* By my soul, he's heard me!

PATHELIN: I'll pretend to be delirious. Now go open the door.

GUILLEMETTE: *[Opening the door]* You're shouting!

DRAPER: And you're laughing! Give me my money!

GUILLEMETTE: Saint Mary! What makes you think I'm laughing? I'd sooner stand on my head. He's passing away. He's nearly gone. You've never heard such an uproar or such a frenzy! He's still delirious! He raves! He chants! And he speaks in all languages! He won't live half an hour. By my faith, it makes me laugh and cry together.

DRAPER: I don't care whether you laugh or cry. To put it briefly, all I want is to be paid.

GUILLEMETTE: Are you mad? Have you started that nonsense again?

DRAPER: I'm not used to this sort of payment for my cloth. Do you think I'm mad? Do you want me to believe that the moon is made out of green cheese?

PATHELIN: *[Delirious]* Come! Stand up! The Queen of Guitars! She'll hurt me if she comes close. I know very well that she's been brought to bed and delivered of twenty-four guitarettes. They're children of the abbot of Yverneaux, so I must be their godfather.

GUILLEMETTE: Ohhh! Think of God the Father, my love, not about guitars.

DRAPER: What's this cock and bull story? Come along, quickly now, I demand to be paid, in gold or silver, for the cloth you've taken.

152   The Farce of Master Pierre Pathelin

GUILLEMETTE: Good Lord! You've already made one mistake. Isn't that enough?

DRAPER: Did you understand me, my good woman? Before God, I don't know what's wrong. I don't even seem to know right from left any longer. Is it unjust for me to demand my money? Eh? By Saint Peter of Rome, I'll . . .

GUILLEMETTE: Alas, how you torment the man! I can see quite clearly in your face that you're not in your right mind. If I were as strong as a fisherwoman I'd tie you up. You're totally mad!

DRAPER: I insist upon my money!

GUILLEMETTE: Ha! That's a nice way to act! Cross yourself in contrition! *[She makes the sign of the cross to him]* Make the sign of the cross! Benedicte!

DRAPER: For gold I'll cross myself! *[Draws back from the writhing Pathelin]* What a sickness this is!

PATHELIN: *[In exaggerated French]*
    Mere de Dieu, la coronade,
    Par ma fye, y m'en vuol anar,
    Or regni biou, oultre la mar!

GUILLEMETTE: He had an uncle in Limoges . . . the brother of his good aunt. That's why he's raving with a Limosin accent.

DRAPER: My God! He's leaving this world with my cloth bundled under his arm.

PATHELIN: *[In burlesque French accent]*
    Where are you going my sweet damiselle?
    And what is that old crapaudaille?
    Go through the rear, merdaille!
[He hides under the covers]

GUILLEMETTE: Ohhh! Alas! The hour approaches when he should be given the last sacrament!

DRAPER: How does he come to speak the dialect of Picardy?

GUILLEMETTE: His mother came from Picardy, and for that reason he still speaks it.

PATHELIN: *[To the Draper, in burlesque German]*
    Wo windest du, mine liebling?
    Du war jung, hubsch, und blond!
    Und now your figure's going,
    But your presence lingers on.

DRAPER: What's this? He never stops. . . . And why in so many languages? Just give me my money, as he promised me, and I'll leave.

GUILLEMETTE: By the tears of God! I'm tired! You're a strange man. What do you want? I don't know anyone as obstinate as you are!

PATHELIN: *[In burlesque French accent]*
Oh, look, there's Reynard in a tub,
Not on the greensward, there's the rub!
He doesn't resemble a cock on the grass,
Not a little mouse or a great jackass!
Call Saint Michael, for I'm dying!

DRAPER: How can he manage to keep on speaking? *[Pathelin becomes frenzied]* Ha! He's going mad in a Norman accent!

GUILLEMETTE: His schoolmaster was a Norman. I supposed he picked up the language from him. Oh, he's sinking fast!

DRAPER: By the good Saint Mary, this is the strangest thing I've ever run across. I'd never have doubted that I saw him this morning at the market.

GUILLEMETTE: Now do you believe me?

DRAPER: Saint John, behold! I don't know what to believe.

PATHELIN: *[Mimes listening]* Is it an ass that I hear bray? *[To the Draper]*
Alas, alas, cousin of mine!
Great sorrow will befall me this day,
I'll no longer see you,
The sun will not shine!
Alas, alas, for I must hate you
Miserable trickster you are, beside.
May you be over-run with lawyers,
Who take your gold out of your hide!

GUILLEMETTE: *[To Pathelin]* God help you!

PATHELIN: Apogee, filagree, masquerade,
Ipso facto coronade.
Munn die filet en cannonade,
Muss-i-den-zumm promenade.

DRAPER: For God's sake, listen to that! He's going. He's rattling in his throat. I wonder what the devil he was babbling about. Sacred Mother! What a mess! By God's body, he sputtered out his words as if he didn't even know what he was talking about. What he was speaking wasn't Christian, or any language I've ever heard of.

GUILLEMETTE: He's dying! He must receive the last sacrament.

PATHELIN: *[To the Draper]*

Hi! By Saint Gigon, you're rich!
Eyes of God! There stands a witch.
Father you're beloved by all,
Rhodomontade about the ball,
Sinking finally out of sight,
In the sunshine of the night.
Straight way down a crooked lane,
Sailing over the sunburned main,
I met a bark who dogged at me;
Meow. Meow. One, two, three.
Stand fast, or by Green George the saint,
I'm sinking! Falling! God, I'm faint!

GUILLEMETTE: By my soul, he's dying as he talks. How he froths at the mouth. Don't you see how he calls upon God? He is going, losing his life, and I'll be left to mourn, poor and unhappy!

DRAPER: *[Aside]* It would be better if I leave before he passes away entirely. *[To Guillemette]* I don't think he'll want to confess his sins in front of me. He'll have secrets, perhaps. Pardon me. I swear to you that I was certain he had my cloth. Adieu, lady. For God's sake, pardon me.

GUILLEMETTE: Blessed be this time you're giving, though not to his sorrowing wife.

DRAPER: *[Aside]* By gentle Saint Mary, I'm puzzled out of my mind. If it wasn't him then it must have been the devil who took my cloth. Benedicite! *[Crossing himself]* He's never bothered me before. And if *he* took it, for God's sake, he can have it! *[He leaves]*

PATHELIN: *[Calling in a low voice]* Come here! What do you think about that? Good riddance to sweet Guillaume. God! Now his head will be filled with nonsense. What dreams he'll have tonight when he goes to bed!

GUILEMETTE: What an insignificant man he is. Didn't you think I played my part well?

PATHELIN: By heaven, you did very well, and as a result we have cloth enough to make clothes for both of us.

V

The Draper's House

DRAPER: What rotten luck! I'm surrounded by liars! I'm soaked in them! They take my merchandise and then they want to take what little I have left. I'm the very King of the

The Farce of Master Pierre Pathelin 155

Unfortunates! The shepherds of the fields cheat me, even my own shepherd to whom I've always been decent. But he's not going to get the better of me. I'm not one of the Fathers of Charity, by Heaven!

[The Shepherd enters]

SHEPHERD: God give you a good day and a good evening, my good master!

DRAPER: Ha! It's you, is it, you nasty rogue! You're a fine servant, you are! What are you up to?

SHEPHERD: I don't want to cause you any displeasure, but it's about what a type of man just said to me. He had stripped clothes, and he was sort of messy, and he had a whip in his hand. He said to me . . . I'm sorry, I don't remember, to tell the truth, even a little bit. He said a lot about you, my master, and something he called, I don't know, a summons. Well, how could I know, by Saint Mary, what it was all about. He was full of grit and said something about going to court this afternoon. . . . Oh, and he made a great to-do about you, master, and what you'd been saying.

DRAPER: I don't know what to say about you before the Judge. I pray to God, may the deluge fall on me, and the tempest! I'll teach you never to beat my sheep; I'll give you a real lesson. I'll see that you pay me for my six yards of cloth . . . I mean, for killing my animals, and for the damage and mischief you've done me over the past ten years.

SHEPHERD: Don't believe those liars, my good master, for by my faith . . .

DRAPER: And, by Our Lady, you'll return it by Saturday. . . . My six yards of cloth! I mean, the sheep you've killed.

SHEPHERD: What cloth? Ha, sir! You mistake me for someone else. By the saints, my master, I'm afraid to say anything when I see you look like that.

DRAPER: Leave me in peace! Go away, and remember to answer the summons. . . .

SHEPHERD: But master, why can't we get together? Before God, what's the use of taking me to court?

DRAPER: Go! Your needs are obvious; go take care of them. I have no need to get together with you. By God, I'll leave your debt for the Judge to decide. If I don't take a strong line about something I shall soon be the laughingstock of the whole village.

SHEPHERD: God bless you, sir, and may He give you joy. *[Aside]* I'd better see about getting someone to defend me.

VI

Pathelin's House

SHEPHERD: *[Knocking at the door]* Is anyone home?
PATHELIN: *[Softly]* He's back! They'll hang me by the neck!
GUILLEMETTE: *[Softly]* What! Not that! By the good and great Saint George, don't let anyone worse come! Get back into bed!

[Guillemette answers the door]

SHEPHERD: God be with you.
PATHELIN: *[From inside the house]* That isn't the Draper's voice. *[Calls out]* God save you, my friend. What's your problem?

[Pathelin appears in the doorway]

SHEPHERD: They'll find me guilty if I don't answer a summons to court. Will you come sir, if you please, and defend me, for I know nothing about these things. I've money to pay you, sir, though I know that my clothes aren't much.
PATHELIN: Come here and tell me, who are you? Are you prosecuting or defending?
SHEPHERD: If I make little sense, listen closely, my good sir. I've looked after his sheep for some years now, and I've guarded them carefully. By my faith, I tell you, he didn't pay me much, but . . . Shall I tell you everything?
PATHELIN: Yes, of course. To your counsel you must tell the whole story.
SHEPHERD: I'll tell you truly, sir. I had to beat these sheep of his so much that several of them fell dead, strong and healthy as they were. I thought he might blame me, sir, and so I told him that they had died of scab. "Ha," he said, "don't leave the diseased ones with the others. Throw them away." "I will," I said, "by Saint John." But I didn't do as he meant. They weren't sick, those sheep, so I ate them. Now let's see. What else? You see, sir, I've been doing this for such a long time, and I've beat and killed so many, that he began to suspect me. He set up a watch, and when I beat the beasts you could hear them cry from

	quite a ways. So I was caught red-handed and I can't deny it, sir. So if I give you some money, master—I've got some, you know—can't we manage to figure out something between us? I know that he's got good cause, but if you put your mind to it I'm sure that you could best him.
PATHELIN:	By my faith, I believe I could get you free. What will you give me if I reverse justice on your accuser and get you acquitted?
SHEPHERD:	I won't even pay you in sous, but in fine gold crowns.
PATHELIN:	I'll build you an excellent case, even though it started out twice as weak. The stronger an opponent's case is, the worse I make it appear when I state my side. Let him tell his story and I'll find a rebuttal that'll make him think twice. Now, listen closely. You're smart enough to understand me, I think. What's your name?
SHEPHERD:	It's Thibaut L'Agnelet.
PATHELIN:	L'Agnelet, have you stolen many a ewe-lamb from your master?
SHEPHERD:	On my oath, I think I've eaten about thirty in the last three years.
PATHELIN:	I suppose that you thought of them as your Christmas presents. Ah, I think it'll work out very well. *[After a short pause]* Oh, by the way, do you think he'll be able to find any unexpected witnesses to testify to his facts? It's very important.
SHEPHERD:	Testify to them, sir? Saint Mary! By all the saints of paradise, he'll find at least ten to testify against me.
PATHELIN:	He has a case that can be made very strong. Still, here's the plan. First, I'll pretend that I don't know you. That I've never seen you before....
SHEPHERD:	Don't do that! God!
PATHELIN:	*[Thoughtfully]* No, nothing will happen. But you must follow the plan. If you speak they'll make you contradict yourself, and in such cases self-confessions are prejudicial and do such great harm that it's the very devil! Therefore, this is what you must do. When you're called to appear for examination and judgment, you must say nothing but "Baaa," no matter what is said to you; and if they start to insult you and say "Ha! You're a barefaced liar, God will punish you, ruffian," or even worse, if they ask you "Do you mock the court?" you must answer "Baaa." Then I'll say, "Ha! He's an idiot. He thinks that he's speaking to his beasts." So, even if they burst with anger, you still don't say anything. And you must be very careful.

158   The Farce of Master Pierre Pathelin

SHEPHERD: It'll be difficult, but I'll truly be careful and I promise to do what you say.

PATHELIN: Be careful. Keep your mouth closed. And remember that whatever I say, don't answer with anything else but "Baaa."

SHEPHERD: Me? No, by my faith! Call me whatever name you will, you or anyone else, and I'll only answer "Baaa." That's a promise.

PATHELIN: By Saint John, thus we'll seize your adversary by the marrow of his bones! And don't forget, I don't want to wait for my money when it's due.

SHEPHERD: Good sir, if I don't pay you as you deserve, then never trust me again. But, I pray you, be diligent with my case.

[A clock strikes]

PATHELIN: By our Lady of Boulogne, I know that the Judge is always seated by six o'clock or thereabouts. You come after me. You understand that we mustn't be seen together.

SHEPHERD: That's good. We don't want people to know that you're my counsel.

PATHELIN: And by our Lady, you'll laugh out of the other side of your mouth if you don't pay up plentifully.

SHEPHERD: My God! At your very word, good sir, truly! Never doubt it. *[He leaves]*

PATHELIN: *[Alone in the street]* Well, well! It doesn't rain money, but it begins to shower. If all goes well I'll see the gleam of gold, and even if the case is worthless I'll get a crown or two for my trouble.

VII

At the Courthouse

PATHELIN: *[Saluting the Judge]* Sir, God give you good health and grant your heart's desire.

JUDGE: You're welcome, sir. Cover yourself and take your place.

[Pathelin sits down and replaces his hat]

PATHELIN: I'm very well here, under your grace. I'm here to seek deliverance.

[The Draper enters the courtroom]

The Farce of Master Pierre Pathelin 159

JUDGE:	If anyone has business, then get it over early so that I can adjourn.
DRAPER:	My counsel is coming, sir. He had a little business to finish, sir, and, if you please, you should wait for him to arrive.
JUDGE:	Well! I have other cases to hear. If your party is present, let's have your story without more stalling. Are you the plaintiff?
DRAPER:	I am.
JUDGE:	Where is the defendant? Is he present in person?
DRAPER:	*[Pointing to the Shepherd]* There he is, the one who says nothing. . . . But God knows that he's thinking.
JUDGE:	Then since you are here, you two, state your case.
DRAPER:	Very well, this is my case against him. Sir, it's the truth before God and in charity that I've taken care of this man ever since he was a child. When I saw that he was strong enough to work in the fields, in short, I made him my shepherd and put him in charge of my sheep. But also, as true as you're sitting there, Master Judge, he has made such a deluge of slaughter among my sheep that without doubt . . .
JUDGE:	Tell me, did you pay him wages?
PATHELIN:	*[Speaking up]* Truly, because if it were learned that he tended them without wages . . .
DRAPER:	*[Recognizing Pathelin]* I disavow God if it isn't you! You without doubt!

[Pathelin tries to hide his face]

JUDGE:	Why are you holding up your hand so high? Do you have a toothache, Master Pierre?
PATHELIN:	Yes! Not even at war have I known such raging pain. I can't even riase my head. For God's sake, let's get on with it.
JUDGE:	*[To the Draper]* Go on! Finish your plea. Quick! End it simply.
DRAPER:	It's him without doubt! Truly! By Christ's cross! It is you to whom I sold six yards of cloth, Master Pierre.
JUDGE:	*[To Pathelin]* Why is he talking about cloth?
PATHELIN:	He's confused. He thinks he is making his case, but he hasn't the ability to do so clearly.
DRAPER:	*[To the Judge]* May I be hanged by the neck if it wasn't him who took my cloth.
PATHELIN:	Where will this evil man go next to find some lie to build up his libel? He means to say—he's such a rascal—that his

shepherd sold some wool, insofar as I understand him, from which the cloth of the clothes that I am wearing was made. He says that this man stole some wool from his sheep.

DRAPER: *[To Pathelin]* Evil creature! I ask God if you haven't got it.

JUDGE: Peace! By the devil! You're slandering! Stop wandering, man. Can't you tell your story without taking up the court's time with so much nonsense?

PATHELIN: I'm so innocent that I can't help laughing. He's made such a mess of his tale that we'd best help him back to the point.

JUDGE: Well! Return to the sheep. What happened to them?

DRAPER: Sir, he took six yards, at nine francs.

JUDGE: Are we simpletons or fools? Six yards of sheep? Do you know where you are?

PATHELIN: By the sacred blood, he thinks you're some animal. He's a good man, from his appearance, but I propose to examine for the party accused.

JUDGE: You speak well. *[Aside]* They are consulting together. They must be at least slightly acquainted. *[To the Shepherd]* Come here. Speak....

SHEPHERD: Baaa.

JUDGE: What's this? Is it "Baaa" that you said? Am I a goat? Speak to me!

SHEPHERD: Baaa.

JUDGE: God's blood, are you mocking me?

PATHELIN: Perhaps he's a fool or stupid. Or, does he think that he's among his animals?

DRAPER: *[To Pathelin]* I know that it was you, and no other, who took my cloth! *[To the Judge]* You don't know, sir, by what malice....

JUDGE: What! Be quiet! Are you mad? Leave this other matter in peace and get back to the main case.

DRAPER: Certainly, sir. But this case has made me so angry that, by my faith, my mouth can't say a single word about it. *[Aside]* If I leave it until another time he'll get away with it by one means or another, and I'll be left to my sorrow. *[To the Judge]* I told you, in my brief, how I gave him six yards ... I mean, ewes ... I pray you, sir, pardon me. This fine fellow ... my shepherd, when he should have been in the fields ... He told me that I would be paid six gold crowns when I came.... What I mean to say is that

The Farce of Master Pierre Pathelin 161

	three years ago my shepherd agreed to look after my sheep and do me no mischief or villainy. But now he truly ... *[To the Judge]* This rascal here stripped the wool from the sheep and killed them by beating their skulls in with a big stick.... When he had my cloth under his arm he rushed out in the street and told me to come and get the six crowns at his house.
JUDGE:	There's neither rhyme nor reason in anything that you say. What is all this? You mix one thing up with another. Sum it all up, by the sacred blood, for I can't judge this. *[To Pathelin]* He raves about some cloth and then babbles about ewes. It's all mixed up. Nothing he says makes sense.
PATHELIN:	I think the trouble is that he's holding back the poor shepherd's wages.
DRAPER:	By God, you'd better be silent! You have my cloth, as true as the Mass. I want my cloth! I know well enough where the shoe pinches, and I know that it was you and no one else. By God, you have it!
JUDGE:	What does he have?
DRAPER:	Nothing, sir! On my oath, he's the most miserable cheat.... Stop! I'll try as best I can not to speak anymore, no matter what happens.
JUDGE:	No, for you might forget. Now, conclude your evidence.
PATHELIN:	The shepherd can't respond to the allegations because he doesn't have counsel and he has no idea of what to ask. If you will please order me to assist him, I'll be glad to do so.
JUDGE:	Assist him? I doubt that it'll be worth your trouble. From his looks there won't be any profit in it.
PATHELIN:	I swear to you that I don't want to make a profit out of it, for God's sake. I'll just find out what the poor fellow can tell me, and then I'll be able to instruct him on how to answer the accusations of his accuser. He'll have trouble making himself understood if he doesn't get help. *[To the Shepherd]* Come here, my friend, I want you to tell me something.... Understand?
SHEPHERD:	Baaa.
PATHELIN:	What does "Baaa" mean? By the sacred blood that God shed, are you mad? Tell me what happened.
SHEPHERD:	Baaa.
PATHELIN:	What's this baaaing? Do you hear ewes bleating? These questions are for your own good. Do you understand?

162   The Farce of Master Pierre Pathelin

SHEPHERD: Baaa.
PATHELIN: What! Answer yes or no. *[Softly]* That's very good. Keep it up. *[Aloud]* Well?
SHEPHERD: *[Softly]* Baaa.
PATHELIN: Louder, or you'll find yourself in great trouble, without a doubt.
SHEPHERD: *[Loud]* Baaa.
PATHELIN: Why, sir, he's even more of a fool than the mad fellow who brought a case against him. Send him back to his ewes. He's a natural-born fool.
DRAPER: He's a fool? By the Lord, he's sharper than you are!
PATHELIN: *[To the Judge]* Send him back to guard his beasts without delay; and may he never return. The plague fall on people who bring charges against such fools.
DRAPER: *[To the Judge]* Is he to be returned before I finish my case?
JUDGE: Good God! Since he's a fool, yes. Why not?
DRAPER: But sir, you must let me have my say and conclude my case. These are not lies that I'm telling, or mockeries.
JUDGE: Those who argue with foolish men and women are all idiots. Listen! If you go on with this rubbish I will recess the court.
DRAPER: You won't hear the case ever again?
JUDGE: And why should I?
PATHELIN: Again! He wants the case to be heard again. *[Speaking of the Shepherd]* You never saw a bigger fool, in what he does and says. *[Of the Draper]* And he's no better than the other. They're both without brains. By the beautiful Saint Mary, there's no difference between them.
DRAPER: You took my cloth by trickery, without paying for it, Master Pierre! I've been victimized! That's not the work of an honest man.
PATHELIN: Really, your honor, if he isn't already mad then he's quickly becoming so.
DRAPER: I know you by your voice and your clothes and your face. I'm not mad! I'm smart enough to know who it is that robbed me! *[To the Judge]* I'll tell you everything, sir, by my conscience!
PATHELIN: *[To the Judge]* Ha, sir! Make him be quiet. *[To the Draper]* Aren't you ashamed to bring charges against this shepherd for three of four old ewes or sheep that aren't worth two buttons? *[To the Judge]* He sings such a sad song....

DRAPER:	What sheep? That's an old one! It's you I'm talking to, and you'll give me back my cloth or, by the God who made us...
JUDGE:	Still talking! Am I in my right mind? Will he never stop braying?
DRAPER:	I demand that you...
PATHELIN:	Make him shut up. *[To the Draper]* By God, you babble too much! What if he did kill six or seven sheep—or a dozen—and ate their carcasses? It's just too bad for you. You've had more than their worth for the time he's been minding them for you.
DRAPER:	You see that? You see? I talk to him about cloth and he answers about sheep. *[To Pathelin]* Six yards of cloth! Where are they? You took them away under your arm. Do you think that you won't have to give them back to me?
PATHELIN:	*[To the Judge]* Would you hang the poor man for the wool of six or seven beasts? *[To the Draper]* Try to restrain yourself. Don't be so hard on that poor, sad shepherd who's as defenseless and as harmless as a worm.
DRAPER:	Then he's the worm who turned! The devil himself must have made me sell cloth to such a sly rogue. *[To the Judge]* Sir, I demand you...
JUDGE:	I have heard your demand and your charges. It's a fine thing to prosecute an imbecile! *[To the Shepherd]* Go back to your sheep.
SHEPHERD:	Baaa.
JUDGE:	*[To the Draper]* You've shown us well the sort of man you are, by the blood of Our Lady!
DRAPER:	But, on my life I only want to...
PATHELIN:	Won't he ever be quiet?
DRAPER:	*[To Pathelin]* It is you I want to get my hands on. You've tricked me and played me false. You've stolen my cloth with your fine speeches.
PATHELIN:	Ha! My conscience is clear. You hear him clearly, sir?
DRAPER:	Good God! You're the biggest rascal... *[To the Judge]* Sir, I tell you...
JUDGE:	This is certainly all very funny. Very entertaining indeed. The two of you together make a most unpleasant sound. *[He rises]* I'm going home. *[To the Shepherd]* Go, my friend, and never return, even if a bailiff summons you to come. The court acquits you. Do you understand?
PATHELIN:	Say "Many thanks."
SHEPHERD:	Baaa.

JUDGE:	Don't I make myself clear? Go! You're free... acquitted....
DRAPER:	But what's the reason that you free him thus?
JUDGE:	*[Dismissing the court]* I've got other business, and your jokes are too much. You make me tired and I'm going home. Will you come and dine with me, Master Pierre?
PATHELIN:	*[Raising his hand to his jaw]* I cannot. My toothache....

VIII

Before the Courthouse

DRAPER:	*[To Pathelin]* Thief! Crook! Tell me, will I ever be paid?
PATHELIN:	For what? Are you going mad? Who do you think I am? By the blood and bones, I think that you have mistaken me for someone else.
SHEPHERD:	Baaa.
PATHELIN:	One moment, good sir. I'll tell you who you have taken me for. Didn't you mistake me for old Brainless? *[Lifting his hat]* See? Isn't he bald on top, just like me?
DRAPER:	Do you take me for a dumb animal? It was you in person; you and no other. Your voice gives you away. It was no one else.
PATHELIN:	Me? No, truly, you have the wrong opinion. Couldn't it have been Jean de Noyon? He's just about my height.
DRAPER:	Ha, devil! He hasn't your drunken face, and he isn't pale from dissipation. Didn't I leave you ill, this morning, in your own house?
PATHELIN:	Ha! That's a nice thing to say. What was the illness? Come, admit your stupidity. *[Reflectively]* Still, it all becomes clear.
DRAPER:	It's you, by noble Saint Peter! It's you and none other. I have no doubt that it's true.
PATHELIN:	Then believe nothing, for it certainly wasn't me. Six yards, you say? I never got a yard from you.... Not even half a yard or anything. How can you bring yourself to say such a thing?
DRAPER:	I'm going to your house, by God's blood, this very minute to see if you're there or not. We can't debate here if you are really there....
PATHELIN:	Do so, by Our Lady! That'll settle the argument.

[The Draper exits]

PATHELIN:	Now, L'Agnelet!
SHEPHERD:	Baaa!
PATHELIN:	Come here. Tell me, did I do well?
SHEPHERD:	Baaa!
PATHELIN:	You can stop that now. There's no need to keep on saying "Baaa" now that you're free. Well, what did you think about it? Was my advice good?
SHEPHERD:	Baaa!
PATHELIN:	Ha! You don't understand. Speak up, no one will hear you.
SHEPHERD:	Baaa!
PATHELIN:	It's time for me to go. Pay me.
SHEPHERD:	Baaa!
PATHELIN:	You played your part perfectly, and what's more, you kept a straight face. That's what finally convinced the Judge. You didn't break down and laugh.
SHEPHERD:	Baaa!
PATHELIN:	What's this "Baaa"? Speak normally, and pay me.
SHEPHERD:	Baaa!
PATHELIN:	What's this? I tell you—I pray you—pay me my money without more bleating, and then be gone. Pay quickly!
SHEPHERD:	Baaa!
PATHELIN:	Are you mocking me? Don't you understand? By my soul, I beg you to pay me without any more bleating. Quickly, my money!
SHEPHERD:	Baaa!
PATHELIN:	You're trying to fool me, isn't that so? I won't go without it.
SHEPHERD:	Baaa!
PATHELIN:	You could twist poetry into prose! Have you forgotten who you're talking to? Do you know who I am? Don't babble to me with your "Baaas." Pay me!
SHEPHERD:	Baaa!
PATHELIN:	You're not going to give me my money? You think that what I did for you was a game? I devoted myself entirely to your defense, as we agreed. Do you think to make me a goose?
SHEPHERD:	Baaa!
PATHELIN:	Ah! You'll make me eat my own goose? *[Aside]* Plague! Am I so old and tired that a shepherd, a sheep in clothes, a nasty rascal can trick me?
SHEPHERD:	Baaa!
PATHELIN:	Don't I have your word? Didn't I appear for you at your

	trial? But, the devil with it. I've had enough argument. Come and dine with me at my house.
SHEPHERD:	Baaa!
PATHELIN:	By Saint John, you have good reason. In the end the young always overtake the old. *[Aside]* I thought I was the master trickster, not only here but in the whole countryside. I was the strongest of bill collectors in collecting on promises of payment. But today a judgment has been rendered and a shepherd has tricked me! *[To the Shepherd]* By Saint James, if I find a bailiff I'll have you taken!
SHEPHERD:	Baaa!
PATHELIN:	Alas! Baaa! Hang me if I don't call a bailiff. And curse him for a fool if he doesn't put you in prison!
SHEPHERD:	*[Running off]* If he catches me, I give him leave!

Suggested Sources For
Readers Theatre Production Material

Once the point has been made—and perhaps belabored—that all literature of all time is fair game for Readers Theatre, it takes a certain amount of cheek to suggest certain authors or works over others. However, for those whose acquaintance with literature is somewhat limited, or for those who just do not have the time to plow through their local libraries seeking out the best and most adaptable authors or works, the following may be of some help. It is, admittedly, incomplete. Still, the range that this listing covers is broad, and it can provide a valuable starting point for further search.

I. BIBLICAL MATERIALS

The Old and New Testaments provide a wealth of material that is highly dramatic and quite adaptable to Readers Theatre. The Old Testament has thirty-nine books, all of which have dramatic possibilities, but of which nine stand out as especially valuable. The New Testament has (generally speaking) sixty-six books, of which fourteen are particularly interesting from a dramatic standpoint and lend themselves easily to a Readers Theatre format.

Old Testament

Exodus
Joshua
Ruth
Ezra
Esther

Job
Psalms
Song of Solomon
Daniel

New Testament

Matthew
Mark
Luke
John
Romans
First Timothy
Second Timothy

Titus
First Peter
Second Peter
First John
Second John
Third John
Jude

II. ESSAYS

The essay is an especially difficult form to adapt to Readers Theatre. Essays must, in most cases, be strung together through some controlling theme or idea. However, a few of the longer essays can stand alone and, delivered properly, can make for an intellectually fascinating program. The following list, in chronological order, spans several hundred years—specifically, from 1545 to 1956. The essays were selected not because they have a common theme, but because they represent some of the best examples of the genre. Some are not essays in the traditional sense, but are selections from longer prose works. They all, however, have in common the ability to stand alone as short, prose disquisitions on particular subjects.

Roger Ascham, *Toxophilus,* "To All Gentlemen and Yeomen of England"
Ben Jonson, *Timber; or Discoveries Made Upon Men and Matter,* "De Style, et Optimo Scribendi Genere"; "Consuetudo"
Francis Bacon, *Essays or Counsels—Civil and Moral,* "Of Truth"; "Of Parents and Children"; "Of Love"; "Of Travel"
John Milton, "Areopagitica"
Jeremy Taylor, *The Rule and Exercises of Holy Dying,* "The Vanity and Shortness of Life"
Jonathan Swift, "A Meditation Upon a Broomstick"; "A Modest Proposal"
Richard Steele, *The Tatler,* "On Ladies' Dress"
Joseph Addison, *The Spectator,* "The Uses of the Spectator"
Samuel Johnson, *The Adventurer,* "The Age of Authors"; *The Idler,* "Of Advertising"
William Wordsworth, "Preface to the *Lyrical Ballads*"
Samuel Taylor Coleridge, *Biographia Literaria,* Chapter XIV
William Hazlitt, "On Familiar Style"; "On Going on a Journey"
Matthew Arnold, *Culture and Anarchy,* "Hebraism and Hellenism"
John Ruskin, *Sesame and Lilies,* "Of Kings' Treasuries"
Walter Horatio Pater, *Studies in the History of the Renaissance,* "Preface"
Washington Irving, *Sketch Book,* "English Writers on America"
Ralph Waldo Emerson, *Essays: First Series,* "Intellect"
Henry David Thoreau, *Walden,* "Solitude"
Mark Twain, "How to Tell a Story"
Henry James, *Essays in London and Elsewhere,* "Criticism"
Aldous Huxley, *Music at Night and Other Stories,* "Selected Snobberies"
George Orwell, *Shooting an Elephant and Other Essays,* "Politics and the English Language"
H. L. Mencken, *A Mencken Chrestomathy,* "American Culture"

Suggested Sources For Readers Theatre Production Material   169

T. S. Eliot, *The Sacred Wood,* "Tradition and the Invidivual Talent"
James Thurber, *The Beast in Me and Other Animals,* "The Waters of the Moon"
E. B. White, *One Man's Meat,* "Dog Training"; "Freedom"
Archibald MacLeish, "Why Do We Teach Poetry?"

III. FOLK MATERIALS

The folk materials on which a Readers Theatre director may draw are enormous. The following list is obviously incomplete and stays within the English/Scottish/American traditions. It includes the "ancient" tales, "Jack" tales, "fool Irishman" tales, "tall" tales, and the ballads (which really *demand* some form of musical presentation). Most of the works mentioned can be found in standard collections of folklore or balladry.

Ancient Tales

Wicked John and the Devil
Mister Fox
The Man in the Kraut Tub
The King and Robert Hood's Horny Beastes
The Big Toe
The Haunted House

Jack Tales

Jack and the Witches
Jack and the Talking Cow
Jack and the Old Strongman

Fool Irishman Tales

Pat and the Mule Eggs
Pat and the Rattlesnake
The Irishman and the Fiddle

Tall Tales

The Split Dog
Old Hide and Taller
The Roguish Cow
Big John Bolling and the Indians

Ballads

Lady Isabel and the Elf-Knight
The Cruel Brother
Lord Randall
Hind Horn
The Marriage of Sir Gawain
The Maid and the Palmer
The Cherry Tree Carol
Bonny Barbara Allen
Dick o' the Cow
Geordie
The Robin Hood Ballads

IV. JOURNALISTIC MATERIALS

It is nearly impossible to list specific materials because it is the very immediacy of such materials that makes them valid. The news stories that, clipped from today's newspaper, make an immediate and valid comment may, by next week, be absolutely dead—and they will almost certainly be dead by next month. Therefore, this section lists a few of those syndicated columnists whose work is not only immediate in its concerns, but written so that it will remain interesting by concentrating on the universal aspects of the "today" situation. This list is obviously very skimpy, but it covers everything from national politics, to sports, to the horrors and humor of everyday housewifery.

Erma Bombeck
Art Buchwald
William F. Buckley

Jim Murray
James Reston
Jack Smith

Suggested Sources For Readers Theatre Production Material

V. NOVELS

It would be hard to imagine a novel that could not, in some way, be adapted to Readers Theatre. Obviously, however, some novels adapt much better than others, if only because in their dialogue or structure or length they present fewer problems to the adapter. The following is hardly exhaustive, but the novels listed cover the whole range of literature—classic, modern mystery, science fiction, and fantasy—and they are all likely prospects for adaptation.

Kingsley Amis, *One Fat Englishman*
Jane Austen, *Pride and Prejudice*
Leigh Brackett, *People of the Talisman*
Charlotte Brontë, *Jane Eyre*
Emily Brontë, *Wuthering Heights*
Daniel Defoe, *Moll Flanders*
Charles Dickens, *Great Expectations*
Theodore Dreiser, *An American Tragedy*
William Faulkner, *The Hamlet*
Henry Fielding, *Tom Jones*
Nathaniel Hawthorne, *The Scarlet Letter*
Ernest Hemingway, *The Sun Also Rises*
Herman Melville, *Billy Budd*
Andre Norton, *Huon of the Horn*
Joyce Porter, *Dover and the Unkindest Cut of All*
Ann Radcliffe, *The Mysteries of Udolpho*
Samuel Richardson, *Clarissa*
John Steinbeck, *Cannery Row*
Mark Twain, *Huckleberry Finn; Tom Sawyer*

VI. PLAYS

The list of plays that would work well in Readers Theatre—that is, with minimal adaptation—is extensive indeed. The following list of twenty plays avoids those great plays (Shakespeare and the Greek classics) that tend to be the common property of all educated people.

Jean Anouilh, *Waltz of the Toreadors*
Bertolt Brecht, *The Good Woman of Setzuan*
Anton Chekhov, *The Cherry Orchard*
T. S. Eliot, *Murder in the Cathedral*

Suggested Sources For Readers Theatre Production Material

Christopher Fry, *The Lady's Not for Burning*
Federico Garcia-Lorca, *The House of Bernarda Alba*
Oliver Goldsmith, *She Stoops to Conquer*
Ben Jonson, *Volpone*
Percy MacKaye, *The Scarecrow*
Christopher Marlow, *The Tragical History of Dr. Faustus*
Arthur Miller, *The Crucible*
Moliere, *The Misanthrope*
Sean O'Casey, *Juno and the Paycock*
Eugene O'Neill, *The Emperor Jones*
Racine, *Phedre*
Jean Paul Sartre, *No Exit*
G. B. Shaw, *The Devil's Disciple*
Oscar Wilde, *The Importance of Being Earnest*
Thornton Wilder, *Our Town*
Tennessee Williams, *The Glass Menagerie*

VII. POETRY

Because of the wide variety of styles, types, and, especially, lengths, poetry has here been subdivided into epic, long, and short works. This is hardly an imaginative, or even traditional, division, but it does provide the Readers Theatre director with a necessary kind of measurement for preparing a program. For the short works it would be particularly absurd to attempt to provide a list of specific poems. To be of any value, such a list would have to be prohibitively extensive. Therefore, "Short Poems" does not provide a list of specific titles, but instead lists those poets whose works might be especially interesting to the Readers Theatre adapter.

Epic

Dante, *The Divine Comedy*
Homer, *Iliad; Odyssey*
Milton, *Paradise Lost*
Vergil, *Aeneid*

Long Poems

Geoffrey Chaucer, *The Canterbury Tales*
Samuel Taylor Coleridge, *The Rime of the Ancient Mariner*

Suggested Sources For Readers Theatre Production Material   173

Hart Crane, *The Bridge*
T. S. Eliot, *The Wasteland*
George Gordon, Lord Byron, *Don Juan*
John Keats, *Lamia; The Fall of Hyperion; The Eve of St. Agnes*
John Milton, *Samson Agonistes*
Alexander Pope, *The Rape of the Lock*
Percy Bysshe Shelley, *Prometheus Unbound*
Edmund Spenser, *The Faerie Queene*
Alfred, Lord Tennyson, *Idylls of the King*

Short Poems

See works by the following:

Matthew Arnold
William Blake
Robert Browning
William Cullen Bryant
George Gordon, Lord Byron
Samuel Taylor Coleridge
E. E. Cummings
Emily Dickenson
John Donne
T. S. Eliot
Robert Frost
Thomas Hardy
Oliver Wendell Holmes
Gerard Manley Hopkins
Ben Jonson
John Keats
Henry Wadsworth Longfellow
James Russell Lowell
Robert Lowell
Archibald MacLeish
John Milton
Edgar Allan Poe
Alexander Pope
Edwin Arlington Robinson
Theodore Roethke
Carl Sandburg
William Shakespeare

Percy Bysshe Shelley
Wallace Stevens
Alfred, Lord Tennyson
Walt Whitman
William Wordsworth
William Butler Yeats

VIII. SHORT STORIES

Nearly any good collection of short stories gives some clues to those writers whose works seem particularly adaptable to Readers Theatre. The following stories are all highly adaptable, are generally available, and include many styles and concerns.

Conrad Aiken, "Mr. Arcularis"
Sherwood Anderson, "Brother Death"
Stella Benson, "The Desert Islander"
Ray Bradbury, "The Last Martian"
A. E. Coppard, "Arabesque: The Mouse"
William Faulkner, "The Bear"
E. M. Forster, "The Celestial Omnibus"
John Galsworthy, "The Apple Tree"
Ernest Hemingway, "My Old Man"; "The Killers"
Aldous Huxley, "The Claxtons"
James Joyce, "A Little Cloud"
Ring Lardner, "Harmony"
D. H. Lawrence, "The Rocking-Horse Winner"
W. Somerset Maugham, "Lord Mountdrago"
Katherine Anne Porter, "Maria Concepcion"
Saki (H. H. Munro), "The Seventh Pullet"
William Saroyan, "The Pomegranate Tree"
John Steinbeck, "Flight"
Edith Wharton, "The Debt"

NOTES TO CHAPTER 1

1. Anton Chekhov, "The Malefactor," trans. and adapted for Readers Theatre by Jerry V. Pickering.
2. *Oral Interpretation,* 3rd ed. (Boston: Houghton Mifflin Company, 1965), Preface, p. v.
3. "Scene Location in Readers Theatre: Static or Dynamic?", *The Speech Teacher,* XIV (September, 1965), p. 193.
4. *The Art of Interpretation* (New York: Holt, Rinehart and Winston, Inc., 1966), p. 311.
5. *Readers Theatre Handbook* (Glenville, Illinois: Scott, Foresman and Company, 1967), pp. 9-10.
6. "Readers Theatre: Some Questions and Answers," *Dramatics,* XXXIV (December, 1962), p. 14.
7. "Readers Theatre as Defined by New York Critics," *The Southern Speech Journal,* XXIX (Summer, 1964), pp. 288-302.

NOTES TO CHAPTER 2

1. For a firsthand discussion of the conception and playing of this work, see Agnes Moorehead's "Staging *Don Juan in Hell*" *Western Speech Quarterly,* XVIII, 3 (May, 1954), pp. 163-66.
2. *Ibid.*
3. *Saturday Review,* 36 (March, 1955), pp. 34-35.
4. *Saturday Review,* (April 7, 1956).
5. Arthur Gelb, "Campaigner in the Cause of Sean O'Casey," *New York Times,* (September 25, 1960), Sect. D, p. 1.
6. *New York Times* (March 30, 1961), p. 25, col. 1.
7. *Theatre Arts,* 44 (June, 1960), pp. 24-50.
8. *New York Times* (September 30, 1963), p. 23, col. 2.
9. *New York Times* (November, 1963), p. 26, col. 1.
10. Alan A. Stambusky, "American College and University Play Production: 1963-64," *Educational Theatre Journal* (May, 1965), pp. 122-27.
11. Alan A. Stambusky, "The 'America First' Attitude in U.S. College and University Play Selection: A Five-Year Report," *Educational Theatre Journal* (May, 1966), pp. 136-39.
12. Leighton M. Ballew and Gerald Kahan, "The AETA Production Lists Project Survey, 1967-68: Minor Variations on Established Themes," *Educational Theatre Journal* (October, 1969), pp. 333-340.
13. Leighton M. Ballew and Gerald Kahan, "The AETA Production Lists Project Survey: 1968-69," *Educational Theatre Journal* (October, 1970), pp. 301-07.

NOTES TO CHAPTER 3

1. Joanna Hawkins Maclay, *Readers Theatre: Toward a Grammar of Practice* (New York: Random House, 1971), p. 7.
2. Maclay, p. 8.
3. Gil Lazier, "Living Newspaper 1970: Obituary for a Gentle Agit-Prop Play," *American Theatre Journal* (May, 1971), pp. 135-151.
4. Coger and White, p. 21.

5. Joseph Conrad, "Youth," in *Masters of the Modern Short Story*, ed. by Walter Havighurst (New York: Harcourt, Brace and Company, 1945), p. 33.
6. Ernest Hemingway, "Ten Indians," in *Reading Modern Short Stories*, ed. by Jarvis A. Thurston (Chicago: Scott Foresman and Company, 1955), p. 171.

NOTES TO CHAPTER 4

1. Aeschylus, "Agamemnon," trans. by E. D. A. Morshead, in *Harvard Classics*, 8, Nine Greek Dramas (New York: P. F. Collier & Son Company, 1909), p. 7. Italics are my own.
2. Christopher Marlowe, *Edward the Second*, ed. by W. Moelwyn Merchant (New York: Hill and Wang, 1967), p. 19.
3. Eugene O'Neill, *Long Day's Journey Into Night* (New Haven: Yale University Press, 1955), p. 58.
4. L. N. Andreyev, "The Seven That Were Hanged," in *Best Russian Short Stories*, ed. by Thomas Seltzer (New York: The Modern Library, 1925), pp. 348-49.

NOTES TO CHAPTER 5

1. Alexander Dean, *Fundamentals of Play Directing*, rev. by Lawrence Carra (New York: Holt, Rinehart & Winston, Inc., 1965), p. 254.

NOTES TO CHAPTER 6

1. Lajos Egri, *The Art of Dramatic Writing* (New York: Simon and Schuster, 1946), p. 3.
2. The concept of rising action, climax, and falling action is based on the work on the nineteenth century German critic, Gustav Freytag.
3. Oscar Wilde, *The Importance of Being Earnest*, reprinted in *Nineteenth Century British Drama*, ed. by Leonard R. N. Ashley (New York: Scott, Foresman and Company, 1967), p. 591.

NOTES TO CHAPTER 7

1. Joanna Hawkins Maclay, *Readers Theatre: Toward a Grammar of Practice* (New York: Random House, 1971), p. 15.

NOTES TO CHAPTER 8

1. Coger and White, *Handbook*, p. 52.
2. Masami Kuni, narration to his film, *A History of Modern Dance*, 2 reels.
3. Francis Hodge, *Play Directing* (Englewood Cliffs, New Jersey: Prentice-Hall, Inc., 1971), p. 92ff.

Index

Action, 46, 47, 55
Act Without Words, 46
Advantages of Readers Theatre, 43-45
Adventures of Huckleberry Finn, The, 26
Aeschylus, 28, 33
Agamemnon, 33
Ages of Man, The, 6
Aidman, Charles, 11, 13
Albee, Edward, 15, 60
Albertson, Jack, 11
Alice in Wonderland, 20
Allen, Clark, 12
Allen, Fred, 24
Allen, Rae, 10
American Theatre Association, 15
Amis, Kingsley, 25, 37
Analysis, 52
An American Tragedy, 84
Anatol, 44, 75
Anderson, Judith, 9
Andreyev, L. N., 38
Animal Farm, 16
Anouilh, Jean, 63
Aristotle, 30, 48
Ash Wednesday, 41
Atmosphere, 79
Audience, 19-20

Babylon Revisited, 25
Bacon, Wallace, 5
Ball, William, 10
Barabbas, 35
Battle of the Sexes, The, 15
Bare, The, 25
Beckett, Samuel, 35, 46
Benét, Stephen Vincent, 6, 9, 15, 23
Bentley, Eric, 11
Bernhardt, Sarah, 60
Bielenberg, John, 5
Blocking, 76
Body responsiveness, 61
Boyer, Charles, 5, 8, 9
Bradbury, Ray, 15, 23, 39, 54
Brecht, Bertolt, 6, 11, 12, 54, 84
Brecht on Brecht, 12, 13, 23
Brenlin, George, 10
Brook, Peter, 21
Brooks, Keith, 5
Byron, George Gordon, Lord, 23

Canterbury Tales, 23
Capote, Truman, 24
Casting by gender, 59
Casting sheet, 63ff
Celestial Omnibus, The, 24
Character, 46, 48-49
Character analysis, 56
Characterization, 26-27
Chaucer, Geoffrey, 23
Chekhov, Anton, 1
Childe Harold's Pilgrimage, 23
Chorus, 97
Christmas Memory, A, 24
Clark, Dane, 12
Climax, 49-50, 55
Coger, Leslie I., 5, 25, 73
Collected short works, 39-41
Collections of short materials, 23
Completeness, 29-30
Composition, 76
Conflict, 49
Congreve, William, 61
Conrad, Joseph, 29, 89
Controlling idea, 53-54
Cooke, Alan, 11
Corwin, Norman, 11, 12, 15
Costigan, James, 24
Costume, 7, 89-90
Cotsworth, Staats, 10
Count of Monte Cristo, The, 28
Crisis, 55

Dandelion Wine, 15, 23, 39
Davis, Bette, 11, 12
Dean, Alexander, 50
Dear Liar, 13
Death of a Salesman, 54
Defender of the Faith, 25
Denouement, 50
Dickens, Charles, 6, 26
Disadvantages of Readers Theatre, 43-45
Dodson, Jack, 10
Don Juan, 23
Don Juan in Hell, 5, 8, 90
Do Not Go Gentle Into That Good Night, 89
Dos Passos, John, 11
Double plot, 48
Doubling, 59

177

178   Index

Doyle, Sir Arthur Conan, 49
Dracula, 23, 79
Dramatic action, 27-28
Dreiser, Theodore, 84
Dress rehearsals, 98-99
Dr. Faustus, 59
Drums Under the Window, 10, 11
Duberman, Martin, 13, 15
Dumas, Alexandre, 28
Dylan, 23

Ebony Ghetto, 15
Edward the Second, 34
Egri, Lajos, 53
Elcar, Dana, 10
Elijah, 78, 84
Eliot, T. S., 15, 16, 17, 25, 27, 40, 41, 44, 54
Elston, Robert, 13
Emotional response, 25
Emperor Jones, The, 18, 83, 85, 89
Endgame, 35
Entrances, 85-87
Essay on Man, 21
Eumenides, 28
Exits, 85-87
Explicating the script, 53

Facial mobility, 61
Falling action, 55
Farewell to Arms, 37
Faulkner, William, 25
Fielding, Henry, 15, 37
First drama quartet, 8, 9
First Nighter, 36
Fitzgerald, F. Scott, 25
Flat characters, 48
Focus, 68-72
Focus (mixed), 71
Focus (offstage), 69-70
Focus (onstage), 69
Follies, 60
Forster, E. M., 24, 48
For Whom the Bell Tolls, 28
Foster, Gloria, 13
Four Quartets, 25, 41
Frankel, Gene, 12
Frankenstein, 23
Freytag, Gustav, 50, 55

Garrett, Betty, 13
Genet, Jean, 60
Gerontion, 27
Gerringer, Robert, 10
Getting Married, 46
Ghelderode, Michel de, 35
Gideon of Scotland Yard, 37

Gielgud, Sir John, 6
Great chain of being, 54
Greene, James, 13
Gregory, Paul, 7, 8
Gunn, Moses, 13

Hamlet, 33, 45
Hardwicke, Sir Cedric, 5, 8
Hearing how lines work, 57
Heart of Darkness, 89
Heckart, Eileen, 11
Hedda Gabler, 60
Hemingway, Ernest, 24, 25, 28, 29, 37, 38, 39, 79
Hicks, Helen, 15
Hills Like White Elephants, 79
Hirshorn, N. C., 13
Hodge, Frances, 77
Hollow Men, 41
Homecoming, The, 78
Home, 84
Hughie, 26, 35
Hugo, Laurence, 11
Humphries, William, 25

Idiot's Delight, 49
I Knock at the Door, 10, 11
Iliad, 84
Importance of Being Earnest, The, 57, 79
Interpretation interest group, 15
Interview (casting), 62
Investigation, The, 14, 17, 39
In White America, 13, 14, 15, 16, 28
Ionesco, Eugene, 35, 48
Irving, Washington, 26

Jackson, Anne, 12
J.B., 15
Job of the Plains, A, 25
John Brown's Body, 9, 11, 15, 16, 23
Journalistic materials, 24, 41

Keeping assignments open, 66
Killers, The, 24
King Lear, 53
King Must Die, The, 26
Kleinau, Marion L., 4
Kleinau, Marvin D., 4
Kuni, Masami, 74

Language, richness of, 28-29
Last Martian, The, 54
Laughton, Charles, 5, 8
Lazier, Gil, 24
Legend of Sleepy Hollow, The, 26
Lenya, Lotte, 12
Lesson, The, 35, 48

Index

Lighting, 7, 88-89
Lindfors, Viveca, 12
Little Moon of Alban, 24
Lollich, LaNor, 17
Long Day's Journey Into Night, 34-35
Lord Mountdrago, 24
Love Song of J. Alfred Prufrock, The, 27, 41
Lucky Jim, 25, 37

McCay, Peggy, 11
Maclay, Joanna Hawkins, 21, 59
Mademoiselle Colombe, 63
Mailer, Norman, 26
Malefactor, The, 1
Male or female?, 59
Marat/Sade, 33
Marco Millions, 45
Marlowe, Christopher, 34, 59
Marric, J. J., 37
Martin, Ross, 11
Massey, Raymond, 9
Masters, Edgar Lee, 13, 15, 23
Maugham, W. Somerset, 24
Me and My Chimney, 26
Medium length prose works, 23-24
Melville, Herman, 26, 37
Merrill, Gary, 11, 12
Miller, Arthur, 54
Milne, A. A., 60
Moby Dick, 37
Molle Mystery Theatre, 36
Mood, 54
Mood (supported by composition), 79
Moon for the Misbegotten, 61
Moorehead, Agnes, 5, 8
Movement, 72-76
Movement (contrasting), 75
Movement (realistic), 75
Movement (result of focus), 74
Movement (suggestive), 74
Mother Courage, 11
Motif, 20-21
Murder in the Cathedral, 41, 44, 54
Music, 7, 89
Musset, Alfred de, 35

Naked and the Dead, The, 26
Narrative materials, 23
Nevins, Claudette, 13
No Excuse, 24
Norris, Frank, 25
No Trifling With Love, 35

Object, sense of, 25
O'Casey, Sean, 6, 10, 11, 13
Octopus, 25

Oedipus at Colonos, 74
O'Neill, Eugene, 18, 26, 34, 35, 45, 61
Oral interpretation, 3
Orwell, George, 16
O'Sullivan, Michael, 13
Our Town, 44

Pantagleize, 35
Participation (audience), 3
Pearlman, Stephen, 13
Performance, 99-100
Period, sense of, 25
Philosophy of Composition, The, 54
Physical relationships, 77
Physical typecasting, 61
Pictures in the Hallway, 10, 11
Pierre Pathelin, The Farce of, 71
Pinkard, Fred, 13
Pinter, Harold, 78
Place, sense of, 25
Plays, 21-22
Play script, 32-35
Plot, 46, 47-48
Poe, Edgar Allan, 54
Point of view, 36
Pope, Alexander, 21
Power, Tyrone, 9
Prometheus Unbound, 23
Prose fiction, 36-39
Psychological relationships of characters, 77

Radio Scripts, 24, 36
Read throughs, 92-93
Redfield, William, 11
Rehearsals (early), 92-94
Rehearsals (final), 98-99
Rehearsals (middle), 94-98
Renault, Mary, 26
Resistible Rise of Arturo Ui, The, 84
Resolution, 49-50
Rice, Elmer, 89
Rising action, 55
Rock, The, 41
Romeo and Juliet, 27, 50, 53, 54
Roth, Philip, 25
Round characters, 48

Sandburg, Carl, 6, 11
Scene changes, 87
Schnitzler, Arthur, 44, 75
Schumann, Walter, 9
Scoring a role, 56
Script, 83
Secret Life of Walter Mitty, The, 24
Setting, 85
Seven That Were Hanged, The, 38

Index

Shakespeare, William, 27, 28, 53, 54, 55
Shaw, George Bernard, 5, 8, 15, 46
Shelley, Percy Bysshe, 23
Sherlock Holmes, 49
Sherwood, Robert, 49
Shyre, Paul, 10, 11, 13
Slice-of-Life, 48
Snows of Kilimanjaro, The, 25
Sondheim, Stephen, 60
Sound, 88-89
Speech Association of America, 15
Spine of the play, 45
Spoon River Anthology, 13, 15, 16, 23, 90
Stage body positions, 80
Stewart, George R., 25
Stoker, Bram, 79
Storm, 25
Street Scene, 89
Subtext, 2
Swiss Family Robinson, The, 27

Tale of Two Cities, A, 26
Technical rehearsals, 98-99
Teitel, Carol, 10
Television scripts, 24
Ten Indians, 29, 38
Tetzel, Joan, 11
Text, 2
Text (onstage), 83
Theatre Group, 11, 13
Theatre Guild on the Air, 36
Theme, 20-21
Thomas, Dylan, 10, 15, 27, 88
Thompson, Sada, 10, 11
Thurber Carnival, A, 15, 16
Thurber, James, 24, 25
... To Meet Mr. Eliot, 23
Tom Jones, 37
Tonality, 62
Tragedy of Tragedies, The, 15

Twain, Mark, 6, 26
Two Evenings with Sean O'Casey, 11
Tynan, Kenneth, 21

Under Milk Wood, 10, 15, 16
Unicorn in the Garden, The, 25
Unity, 29-30
USA, 11, 89

Van Patten, Joyce, 13
Vaughan, Stuart, 10
Vocal range, 62
Voskovec, George, 12

Wagner, Michael, 12
Waiting for Godot, 35
Waiting for Lefty, 27
Warming-up exercises, 96
Wasteland, The, 41
Way of the World, The, 61
Weiss, Peter, 14, 39
What Price Glory, 26
When Lilacs Last in the Dooryard Bloom'd, 25
White, Melvin R., 5, 25
White, Richard, 9, 73
Whitman, Walt, 25
Who's Afraid of Virginia Woolf?, 60
Wilde, Oscar, 6
Wilder, Thornton, 44
Williams, Tennessee, 15
Wind in the Willows, The, 20
Windom, William, 11
Winnie the Pooh, 59
Woffington, Peg, 60
World of Carl Sandburg, The, 11, 12, 13, 15, 16, 89

Youth, 29

DATE DUE			
MAY 19 1983			
GAYLORD			PRINTED IN U.S.A.

WITHDRAWN from the Alma College Library